Marx in Movement

Antonio Negri

Marx in Movement

Operaismo in Context

Translated by Ed Emery

polity

Polity Press
65 Bridge Street
Cambridge CB2 1UR, UK

Polity Press
101 Station Landing
Suite 300
Medford, MA 02155, USA

ISBN-13: 978-1-5095-4423-3 - hardback
ISBN-13: 978-1-5095-4424-0 - paperback

A catalogue record for this book is available from the British Library.

Library of Congress Cataloging-in-Publication Data
Names: Negri, Antonio, 1933- author.
Title: Marx in movement : operaismo in context / Antonio Negri ; translated by Ed Emery.
Description: Cambridge, UK ; Medford, MA : Polity Press, [2021] | Includes bibliographical references. | Summary: "A leading Marxist theorist analyses the changing nature of work"-- Provided by publisher.
Identifiers: LCCN 2021008265 (print) | LCCN 2021008266 (ebook) | ISBN 9781509544233 (hardback) | ISBN 9781509544240 (paperback) | ISBN 9781509544257 (epub) | ISBN 9781509547654 (pdf)
Subjects: LCSH: Marxian economics. | Labor. | Socialism. | Marx, Karl, 1818-1883.
Classification: LCC HB97.5 .N3998 2021 (print) | LCC HB97.5 (ebook) | DDC 335.4/11--dc23
LC record available at https://lccn.loc.gov/2021008265
LC ebook record available at https://lccn.loc.gov/2021008266

Typeset in 10.5 on 12pt Plantin by
Servis Filmsetting Ltd, Stockport, Cheshire
Printed and bound in Great Britain by CPI Group (UK) Ltd, Croydon

For further information on Polity, visit our website: politybooks.com

Contents

Introduction: Marx in *operaismo*, a Long Road   1

Part I   From the Mass Worker to the Social Worker

1   Archaeology and Project: The Mass Worker and the
    Social Worker   11

2   On Recent Trends in the Communist Theory of the State:
    A Critical Review   39

3   Labour Value: Crisis and Problems of Reconstruction in
    Postmodernity   76

Part II   Workers and Capital Today

4   Marx and Labour: The Path to Disutopia   85

5   The Capital–Labour Relationship in Cognitive Capitalism   100
    Antonio Negri and Carlo Vercellone

6   The Organic Composition of Capital Today   111

7   General Intellect and the Social Individual in Marx's
    Grundrisse   122

Part III   Polemical Considerations

8   *Operai e capitale* Fifty Years On: What Has Happened in
    the Working Class since Marx?   143
    Antonio Negri and Mario Tronti

9 On Tronti's Autonomy of the Political   156

10 Post-*operaismo*? No, Just *operaismo*!   166

Notes   177

Introduction

Marx in *operaismo*, a Long Road

In *operaismo* [workerism],* the reading of Marx is done from a particular viewpoint, which is that of the class struggle, and this means that such a reading takes as its starting point the cognitive interest of communist militants involved in the class struggle. Marx is, as it were, an open book from which processes of inquiry [*inchiesta*], theoretical research and political intervention by communists can draw their tools, which change with the passing of time in the long continuity of revolutionary political excavation. In workerism Marx is addressed in an open reading; his books are periodically selected or privileged when they are found to be particularly relevant to the development of the class struggle and to the changes that take place in its composition.

I can start from an set of initial questions. What is workerism's relationship to history? What is the 'historical materialism' of workerism's key writers? The answer is simple: in workerist writings you do not find any teleological, finalist or positivist historicism – the kind of historical view that points to the victory of the working class as necessary, close at hand, and inscribed in the nature of working-class struggle. History is the *historicity* of its subjects, seen as being in a state of continuous transformation, which is based on transformations in living labour – in its relationship with machines and with cooperation; and another thing that needs to be considered is the subjectivation and accumulation of the institutions that represent the composition of the working class at any given time.

---

* Translator's note: For the purposes of this volume I use 'workerism' as a translation of *operaismo* in some chapters, although it has slightly negative overtones in English.

If one relates the practice of this materialist approach to the reading of particular texts by Marx, one finds a shift right at the origins of workerism. At the beginning the tendency was to focus on volume 2 of *Capital*, which analyses the relationship between factory and society and the transition from extraction of surplus value in the factory to its accumulation at the level of social circulation. Then there was a shift to volume 3 of *Capital*, where the analysis moves up, to the level of the abstraction of value and to analysis of globalization; and it was followed by a shift to volume 1 of *Capital*; to the *Grundrisse*, where the historical theme of the subjectivation of struggles is the principal starting point of analysis; and also to the pages of the 'Fragment on Machines', at a point where analysis led to an identification of cognitive labour and general intellect as being central to the mode of production. In this way workerism was able to enrich itself with a number of points of view that were homogeneous, albeit different, and that enabled it to keep up with the historical changes in the nature of the class struggle.

It is with this freedom that, with the passage of time, the whole of Marx's teaching is appropriated by workerist writers and put at the service of struggles. In the nascent phase of workerism, Raniero Panzieri, writing about the concept of social totalization, invokes Lukács against the perversion of Marxian thought represented by the critical theory of the Frankfurt School. Indeed the latter is seen as being engaged in a quest for equilibrium in what was understood as *the plan of capital*. Subsequently Mario Tronti rediscovers and popularizes Marx's inventive concept of class struggle as falling within the concept of capital and of capital's totalization of the social. The concept of capital is understood as the concept of *a relationship* in which living labour prevails as a form of movement within the struggle over exploitation. Struggles are the engine of development, and the counterpower of the working class is the destituent soul [*l'anima destituente*] of all capitalist power and the proletarian constituent power [*potenza costituente*] of all revolutionary production. With Romano Alquati, the process of workers' inquiry gives arms and legs to these early workerist institutions, emphasizing the connection between living labour and the technical composition of capital and beginning to describe analytically the relationship between struggles and machinery in each phase of development of working class subjectivity, while Sergio Bologna and Mauro Gobbini, already in this first cluster of theoretical and political work, are highlighting the form of the relationship that the life and the ethical and ideological–political behaviours of the proletariat (in the social and political composition in which we analyse them) establish with the *technical* dimensions of labour of the proletariat in the history of the struggles. The *political composition* of skilled workers is thus defined in relation to their relative independence of the control exercised by the employer (in the machine system), whereas the (Taylorized) mass worker would be completely crushed in the new *technical composition* of Fordism. In this way, the methodological understandings contained in E. P. Thompson's *Making of the English Working Class* are actualized in the eighteenth- and nineteenth-century transition to the highest and most extreme form taken by industry. All this was in the 1960s.

In the early 1970s a new phase already opens in workerist research, and it is built around the formidably anticipatory work of Maria Rosa Dalla Costa, Alisa Del Re, and other women comrades working on the issue of reproduction. The movement for wages for housework shifts the analysis from the factory to the home, from male workers to their families, and captures, in the social dimension of exploitation, the specificity of the exploitation suffered by woman – as mother, as daughter, as careworker, as first agent of social reproduction. This is an explosive moment in workerist research. In this way workerism comes to be massively a part of *feminism* and, in addition to proposing areas for the liberation of women, it builds those mechanisms of research and critique of the *patriarchal power* that make possible the expansion of the concept of surplus value and exploitation to society as a whole, far beyond the factory. This shift, in turn, makes it possible to widen workerist analysis, extending it from production to reproduction. This then led to a second cluster of studies, accompanied, as always, by experiences of militancy and intervention and exemplified in the work of Luciano Ferrari Bravo, Ferruccio Gambino, Sandro Serafini (and, next, of Karl Heinz Roth and Yann Moulier) on the socialization of living labour and on the mobility of labour power. The radical critique of schemas of reproduction in the light of historical research, the invention of an *alternative* history of the working class, and the revisiting of slavery and colonialism in the light of the development of capitalism thus come to constitute a new terrain of analysis.

By now we have moved definitively beyond some of the Eurocentric limits of the initial programme of theoretical workerism. From the perspective of the work carried out during these years (moving into the 1980s), the workerist analysis indeed broke with the old socialist classification of economic periods and modes of production, tracing a line of development of capitalism that included colonialism and slavery as *determining* and *internal* elements. The critical and subversive analysis of patriarchy had allowed us to view the systemic links of the processes of exploitation and proletarianization 'through command' – and, in this context, to tighten the analysis of the production of goods and of the reproduction of forms of command for social exploitation.

A third phase of workerist development began in the 1980s and 1990s, when Christian Marazzi, Paolo Virno, Maurizio Lazzarato and Carlo Vercellone (among others, and with continuous and bold contributions from Sergio Bologna and the journal *Primo Maggio*) began to investigate the new technical composition of social labour [*lavoro sociale*], starting from the dissolution of Fordism and the birth of neoliberalism and stressing the monetary and financial mediations in post-Fordism, as well as the combined phenomena of *precarization* and the *cognitive figure* of living labour as fundamental elements that characterize the current phase of capitalist development. And then there were the studies of Michael Hardt, Sandro Mezzadra and Brett Neilson on global migration and the international dimension of the class struggle, with multiplications that were now becoming viral.

★ ★ ★

It is within this framework that, in this book, I document my own contribution to the development of workerism, and in particular to the transformation represented in the transition from the mass worker to the social worker [*dall'operaio massa all'operaio sociale*]. I would say that, with my work, I have liberated the method and concept of living labour from the dialectical cages that kept it confined to the factory. In fact it should be noted that, even when the inquiries and the practices of struggle testified to the fact that the front of the class struggle had expanded to other figures of living labour that were extraneous to the factory (women in domestic and care work, ethnic minorities crushed at the bottom of the social hierarchy, students and scientific researchers now subjected to the productive order of capitalism, etc.) – and so even when it seemed that the path to a definition of living labour on the social terrain was finally open – people were not able to imagine the independence of *a new, living figure of living labour*, totally social, whose productive composition was not fixed by belonging to the factory. The reasons for this were an insufficiency of research and a kind of reverential ethical timidity in the face of the glorious tradition of the struggles of factory workers. The situation became more serious when that inability to recognize the new stemmed from a refusal to imagine any 'technical composition' of productive labour other than that which the Third International had proposed for the class as 'political composition' (perhaps correctly in the case of Leninism, but certainly wrongly in Stalinism). In consequence, even when the technical composition of Fordism had come to an end, had exhausted itself, it was still maintained in theory, because people could (and would) not go, in the political sphere, beyond old organizational forms that were the political counterpart of Fordism. What disasters – repressive and reformist – that desire for continuity (or rather for more of the same) had created in the shipwreck of 'real socialism' and its party offshoots! Hence it was only by destroying that identitarian and repressive – let alone mystificatory and reformist – enclave that the irreducibly revolutionary nature of the Marxian definition of the class could be actualized. This meant dissolving the political practice and the ideology of the mass worker and proceeding straight to the analysis of exploitation in the socialization of living labour (e.g. networks of cognitive and care work that subsequently went on to become activist groupings, political platforms). This is the theoretical and practical contribution that, since the 1970s, I have tried to make to the development of class struggles. I think I managed to impose this truth.

★ ★ ★

In the first part of this volume, 'From the Mass Worker to the Social Worker', I offer three articles that illustrate the transition from the first to that second form of technical and political composition of the proletariat, which took place during the 1970s, and my commitment to defining it. 'Archaeology and Project' (1981) summarizes what happened; this piece represents the result of my research in those years. The next article, on how left-wing state theory reacted to the crisis that followed the American administration's decision in 1971 to cancel the Bretton Woods agreements, dates from 1974. It seeks to show how the transformation of production relations had a direct influence on the transformation of the structure of the state and how class struggles (in the transformation of the mass worker into a social worker) profoundly affected the capital relationship and the capitalist composition of society. The underlying critical basis of this piece is a dialogue with the work of Claus Offe, who during those years gives the best of himself to analysing these same questions.

In the initial plan for this volume, three other articles of mine, written in the early years of my involvement in Marxist workerism, were to be included in Part I; these will now be published in the next volume of this collection. Two of them, 'Keynes and the Capitalist Theory of the State' and 'Cycle and Crisis in Marx's *Capital*', are pieces from 1967–8 that illustrate two points of approach in workerist research on the Marxist theory of the state and on the critique of the social market economy. In them I deepen the analysis of the homogeneity and mirroring of the Fordist mode of production, of the Taylorist labour process, and of the Keynesian state machine. The third, 'State, Public Expenditure and the Decline of the Historic Compromise', dates from 1975 and focuses on a topic that was discussed among Marxist theorists in the early 1970s – that is, at a time when the problem of reproduction appeared dramatically as a problem of public debt under the pressure of workers' struggles.

The third and final article in Part I was written in the same period and deals with value theory. It opens to the study of the political practices of the new subjectivities, in other words to counterpower dynamics and to the development of constituent power [*potenza costituente*], practices that bring about the destruction of the relationship of equilibrium that bourgeois political economy prescribes for the extraction of profit. The very possibility of this equilibrium is radically contested here in the name of that theoretical discovery that the struggles of the 1960s and 1970s opened to: *historical verification*. Historical verification consists of the *dispositif* of the constituent cooperation of living labour, a process that had become central to the formation of the social worker. 'From the mass worker to the social worker' [*dall'operaio-massa all'operaio sociale*] can also be expressed as 'from the *self-valorization* of the mass worker to the constituent *cooperation* of the social worker'. It is on this *dispositif* that the new revolutionary power of the cognitive proletariat would subsequently be based; and the cognitive proletariat, by recognizing its own productive autonomy, removes any dialectical link with the command of capital.

★ ★ ★

The title of Part II is 'Workers and Capital Today'. Under this title I gather some materials that I consider important for reading Marx in the current phase of the class struggle.

I begin with a reading of the 'Fragment on Machines'. This is an invitation to accompany the prescient Marx, Marx the futurologist, in recognizing a figure of production and exploitation that we can all see to be present and topical today, after 150 years. The 'Fragment' shows Marx engaged in reading a new era in class struggle and open to a dystopian dimension that we have to transfer critically into our own reality. With this theoretical shift it is possible to arrive at the definition of a new proletarian subject – the *cognitive worker* – who attacks social exploitation in proportion to the development of the mode of production, and yet with renewed power. The Marxian method – as reconstructed in workerism – shows here that it has a dual ability: to destructure the opponent and to find the figures of the to-come [*a-venire*] not in the ruins of power but in the struggle's constituent power [*potenza costituente*].

The second article translated in Part II presents the first original attempt at a cognitive definition of productive social subjectivity in the Marxian ontology of productive labour. This text, produced in the 1990s in collaboration with Carlo Vercellone, opens to the redefinition of labour power as an immaterial, biopolitical *cognitive power*, capable of appearing as power of cooperation – from time to time subjected but also resistant to, constituent of, and alternative to capital exploitation.

The next two articles in Part II are papers delivered at conferences in recent years, one in Paris, the other in Berlin, and they conclude my research on the organic composition (technical and political) of capital and class today. In both, I redefine what it means to practise intervention and investigation from the workers' point of view in today's conditions. The contribution that these texts make to workerism consists, in my view, in highlighting the *ontological basis* of the new productive power of social cooperation and, at the same time, the manner in which the 'social individual' (through whom capital extracts surplus value) has the capability of becoming a political force today. Entirely monistic in Marx's analysis, this nexus of economics and politics seems to constitute an enigma against which many theoretical lines have crashed, but in reality it is nothing but the most constant and determinate index of an immanentist, materialist journey that cannot be abandoned by revolutionaries.

★ ★ ★

Finally I include, as Part III, some materials that arose out of discussions with Mario Tronti and show that, contrary to what he claims, workerism cannot be read solely as his personal experience – a view that led him to assert that workerism came to an end in 1966, with the closure of the journal *Classe operaia*. I argue that workerism continues to exist well beyond that date and can be seen as a powerful instrument of revolutionary theory and practice that develops through new struggles and new inventions today. Is it worth making this claim? Maybe not, if it is true that, after 1966, Tronti spent the rest of his life crying over what he had done as a young man – as Daniel Bensaïd and Étienne Balibar have always maintained. It does not particularly concern me whether this was from nostalgia or from regret: the fate of a person who opened a future of research but then soon retired from the struggles remains pathetic whether he did it from nostalgia or from regret (and I don't care which one it is), especially when he returned to doing political activity in the name of a worn-out tradition and in a party that was responsible for the social–democratic corruption and the present foundering of Italian and European political life. No, militant workerism, which is now a healthy trend among the younger generations, has never been able to live with that degradation. I repeat: the political defeat that workerism suffered in Italy at the end of the 1970s was rather the basis for an expansion of its influence on revolutionary culture worldwide. Workerism will never be a 'post-' phenomenon; it will always be key to understanding class struggle – or rather a new transition, from the *multitude* that lives within the crisis to a *new working class* that is rising up.

Antonio Negri, May 2020

Part I

From the Mass Worker
to the Social Worker

1

Archaeology and Project*

The Mass Worker and the Social Worker

1 Functions and limitations of the concept of the mass worker

In the wake of the 20th Congress of the Communist Party of the Soviet Union in 1956, the critique of Stalinism, which developed within the Italian labour movement above all, put into question the traditional conception of the trade union. This had become an area of key concern. In 1953, there had been a resounding defeat of the communist union at FIAT; in the years that followed, there were equally resounding defeats in line for the farm workers' unions and the public sector unions (railway workers, postal workers etc.). The fading (or downright disappearance) of any immediate prospect of a seizure of power and a series of confusions at the ideological level meant that the trade unions were being undermined as the transmission belt of the system; both their organizational form and their ideological basis were thrown into crisis. But this crisis did not affect the radicality of the working class. There began to appear a mass form of behaviour that was spontaneous, multiform, violent, mobile and disorderly – but that, nonetheless, was able to compensate for the lack of trade union leadership in ways that were both original and powerful – and while

---

* This English translation was originally published in A. Negri, *Revolution Retrieved: Selected Writings on Marx, Keynes, Capitalist Crisis and New Social Subjects, 1967–83*, ed. and trans. by E. Emery and J. Merrington, Red Notes: London 1988, pp. 102–15. Originally published in *Macchina-tempo: Rompicapi, liberazione, costituzione*, under the title 'Archeologia e progetto: L'operaio massa e l'operaio sociale', Feltrinelli: Milan 1982, pp. 149–69.

the union leaderships stuck to a repetition of the old forms, the working class reacted in ways that were autonomous. The union would call strike action and the entire workforce would go in to work – but then, after a week, a month, maybe a year, that same working class would explode in spontaneous demonstrations. The farm workers of the south also began spontaneous struggles. However, they had been defeated in the movement to take over agricultural land; they had been sold out by the government's agrarian reform, which condemned them to the poverty of having to work small holdings. As a result, the rural vanguards chose the path of large-scale emigration. This was a mass phenomenon – its causes and effects were complex, certainly, but its quality was political. Then things began to move: Milan in 1959, Genova in 1960, Turin in 1962, and Porto Marghera in 1963 – a series of struggles that pushed to the forefront of the political scene. This succession of labour struggles involved every major sector of industry and all the major urban concentrations. They were all more or less spontaneous mass events and revealed a degree of general circulation of modes of struggle that had not previously been experienced.

One might well ask for a definition of this spontaneity of the struggles. For, while it is true that the struggles were in large part independent of the control and the command of the trade unions (and the unions were sometimes not even aware of them), at the same time they appeared – and were – *strongly structured*. They revealed the existence of new working-class leaderships that were, as we used to say, 'invisible' – in part because many people simply didn't want to see them, but also (and mainly) because of their mass character, because of the new mechanisms of cooperation that were coming into play in the formation of workers' political understanding, because of the extraordinary ability to circulate of these new forms of struggle, and because of the degree of understanding (of the productive process) that they revealed. And, while these new forms of struggle were at first seen by most people as 'irrational', in the course of their development they gradually began to reveal a coherent project and a tactical intelligence that finally began to problematize the very concept of working-class rationality. Economic rationality? Socialist rationality? Rationality of the law of value? Rationality of trade union control? Rationality of law and order? And so on. In effect, in the form taken by these struggles we could identify elements that were directly contradictory to the whole structure of trade unionist–socialist ideology. The wage demands, and the extremes to which they went, contradicted the way in which, in traditional trade union practice, the wage had been used as a political instrument, as a means of mediation. The partisan nature (egotism) of the struggles ran heavily counter to the socialist ideology of the homogeneity of working-class interests that had prevailed up until then. The immediacy and the autonomous nature of struggles ranging from wildcat strikes to mass sabotage, their powerful negative effect on the structures of the cycle of production, ran counter to the traditional view that fixed capital is sacrosanct, and also counter to the ideology of liberation of (through) work – in which work was the subject of liberation, and Stakhanovism or high levels of professional skill the form of liberation. Finally, the intensification (whether at group or at individual level) of heightened forms of mobility, of absenteeism, of socialization of the struggle, ran immediately counter to any factory-centred conception of working-class interests of the kind that has come down to us from the workers' councilist tradition. All this gradually uncovered, in increasingly socialized forms, an attitude of struggle against work, a desire for liberation from work – whether it be work in the big factory, with all its qualities of alienation, or work in general, as conceded to the capitalist in exchange for a wage.

The paradox of the situation was that this mass spontaneity, highly structured in itself, negated in principle the very definition of spontaneity. Traditionally, spontaneity has been taken to mean a low level of working-class consciousness, a reduction of the working class to simple labour power. Here, though, it was different. This *spontaneity* represented a very high level of class maturity. It was a spontaneous negation of the nature of the working class as labour power. This tendency was clearly present, and later developments were to reveal it still further. Thus anybody who wanted to analyse the new forms of struggle was going to have to be prepared to problematize the entire theoretical tradition of socialism. Within these struggles there were *new categories* waiting to be discovered.

And this is what was done. In the early 1960s, on the fringes of the official labour movement, a number of working-class vanguards and a number of groups of intellectuals active within the class struggle produced a theory in which the mass worker was understood as the new subject of working-class struggles.

On the one hand, their studies identified the *objective* characteristics of this class protagonist. These characteristics were determined as follows:

- within the organization of the labour process, by Taylorism;
- within the organization of the working day and of wage relations, by Fordism;

- within economic–political relations, by Keynesianism;
- within general social and state relations, by the model and the practice of the planner state.

On the other hand, they succeeded in defining (this was absolutely imperative) the new *subjective* characteristics of this new configuration of the class. These subjective characteristics were described in terms that were dynamic and highly productive. In other words, every aspect of the capitalist organization of the factory society was to be seen as the product of a dialectic between working-class struggle and capitalist development (including developments in technology, in the form of the wage, in economic policy, and in the form of the state) – the product of a dialectic whose active and motive central force was the mass worker.

As our old friend Marx says, machines rush to where there are strikes.

All the mechanisms of capitalist control of development were brought to bear at critical points within the system. By means of a continual theft of the information generated by the struggles, capital created increasingly complex mechanisms of domination. It was within this framework that the analysis undertaken by workerism unstitched the capitalist Moloch, following the indications provided by working-class struggle. The comrades arrived at a fundamental theoretical conclusion: that, given a certain level of capitalist development, the concept of labour power (understood as an element of the dialectical relationship between workers and capital, a relationship in which capitalist logic has the upper hand) becomes dissolved. A dialectical relationship most certainly remains, but now the relationship between capital and labour power becomes the relationship of capital with the working class. Thus the dialectic of capitalist development is dominated by the relationship with the working class. The working class now constituted an *independent polarity* within capitalist development. Capitalist development was now dependent on the political variable of working-class behaviours. The concept of labour power could no longer be substantiated; only that of working class was adequate.

I have to admit that our theoretical and political positions in this period, while very rich in some respects, were very poor in others. Their richness lay in the fact that they provided a basis from which we could then develop an entirely political concept of labour power. We learned a lot from developments in the capitalist revolution of the 1930s and 1940s. In particular, we learned that it was possible to carry forward revolutionary struggles that had a marked effect both on the structure of the labour process and on the structure of economic and political domination – in other words, struggles that were capable of winning *against Taylorism* and *within Keynesianism*. On the other hand, the poverty of our theoretical and practical positions lay in the fact that, while individual struggles and the struggles of individual class sectors proved capable of understanding capital and taking it on, at the same time the potential of that struggle, its strategic dimension, and the re-establishment of a centre of revolutionary initiative remained beyond our grasp. Practice, even the highest working-class practice, at this level of the class struggle, always contains an element of uncertainty as regards its synthesis and resolution – what Lenin used to call 'the art of insurrection', an art that the workers today are seeking to turn into science. This science still had to be constructed – a science that the practice of the mass worker was demanding, but that it did not provide.

In fact capital's science of domination was far ahead of us. At the time when we were introducing the concept of the mass worker and, by implication, a critique of the category of labour power in favour of a concept of dynamism of the working class, capital, for its part, had already made tremendous advances in its own practice, as regards its theory of domination and redressing the balance of power. (Note that within the specificities and the isolation of a few national situations – in Italy in particular – we were successful in developing a remarkable level of subjective action and in bringing about moments of deep capitalist crisis.) For, while from the working-class viewpoint the revolutionary practice of the mass worker was being advanced within individual factories and within the overall interlocked system of factories and companies, capital was already responding, generally at the global and social level, with domination and control. Keynesianism, at its roots, had already demonstrated this: an awareness not only that the wage relation extended between subjects that were different (capital and the working class), but above all that the solution (favourable to capitalist development) was to be sought *across the entire span of production and circulation* – in other words, involving the entire sociality of the relations of production and reproduction. In the Keynesian system, state budgeting was the means of recuperating and neutralizing the class struggle in the factory, and monetary policy was the means of subordinating the wage relation. Fordism, for its part, had already transformed the high level of cooperation on the assembly line (and thus corrected those elements of weakness that labour struggles, at that level of production, were able to turn against capitalist command) into a conscious policy, one might say, of the sociality of the assembly line – a policy of command over the relation between industrial production and the reproduction of labour power, a capitalist intervention within the social flexibility of labour power, a way of privileging social command and divisions within society as conditions for command and division on the assembly line. Fordism recuperated social motivations and made them functional to the Taylorist organization of work – it posed them as the prime and fundamental terrain of command in the factory. Gradually the labour market and the fabric of relations between production and reproduction was becoming an operative field (this also from the theoretical point of view) for the capitalist theory of factory command: hence the development from Keynes's to Kaldor's planning techniques to Kalecki's microanalyses of the political cycle and to the present systemic theories of neo-functionalism.

Faced with these developments in capital's understanding of the articulations of command, not only was the concept of the mass worker *late* in developing, but also, crucially, it now proved incapable of developing for itself a theory able to match the new dimensions of command. Of course, the old workerists of the 1960s knew that they had to go beyond the 'empirical' category of the factory and that the mass worker had to become effective over the entire span of the social factory – but the factoryist content of the concept and the circumstances of its genesis prevented its theoretical potential from becoming practical reality. Thus, in the end, this *impotence of the mass worker* left the way open for surreptitious operations of mediation and representation – and the whole old machinery of the party form was wheeled out as the means whereby issues could be posed at the social, political and general level. We should also add (and this is not only of historical relevance) that this was the basis on which the trade union was able to re-establish its powers of control over the working class. This had a paradoxical consequence: the trade union accepted the delegation of power and the general functions that the working class had restored to it, and then went on to impose rules that separated, in a corporatist sense, the working class from the other proletarianized strata of society. When the trade union (in its traditional function, as half party and half merchandiser, in the sense that it represents labour power within the bourgeois political market and also sells labour as a commodity on the capitalist market) finally caught up with and grasped – after '68 – the new composition of the mass worker, it only reduced it to corporatism and divided it from the rest of social labour.

Hence it follows that a methodology such as I use, which seeks to indicate possibilities for subjective genesis within the categories of class struggle, cannot rest content with this old version of the concept of the mass worker. And indeed, the conditions for further theoretical progress on this front were plentiful, especially in the years immediately following the upheavals of 1968–9. Working-class struggles, which were extremely powerful in spite of (or perhaps because of) their ambiguity as struggles both within and against the system of the relative wage, now brought about a crisis in the mechanisms of capitalist control. The capitalist response during this period developed along two complementary lines – the social diffusion and decentralization of production; and the political isolation of the mass worker in the factory.

The only possible answer to this, from the working-class viewpoint, was to insist on and fight for the broadest definition of class unity, to modify and extend the concept of working-class productive labour, and to eliminate the theoretical isolation of the concept of mass worker (insofar as this concept had inevitably become tied to an empirical notion of the factory – a simplified factoryism – owing to the impact of the bosses' counteroffensive, the corporatism of the unions, and the historical and theoretical limitations of the concept itself). On the other hand, the emergence and growth of diffused forms of production (the 'diffuse factory'), while they enlarged the labour market enormously, also redefined, as directly productive and 'working class', a whole series of functions within social labour that would otherwise be seen as marginal or latent. Finally, there was a growing awareness of the interconnection between productive labour and the labour of reproduction, and it was expressed in a wide range of behaviours in social struggles, above all in the mass movements of women and youth, who affirmed all these activities, collectively, as labour. This development made necessary an innovation in the vocabulary of class concepts: as we used to put it, 'from the mass worker to the social worker'. But it would be more correct to say 'from the working class', that is, from that working class massified in direct production in the factory, 'to social labour power', which represented the potentiality of a new working class, now extended throughout the entire span of production and reproduction – a conception more adequate to the wider and more searching dimensions of capitalist control over society and social labour as a whole.

There are numerous problems that arise at this point, and I have no intention of trying to avoid them. In what follows I hope to confront at least some of them. It will suffice at this stage to introduce what I consider to be the key methodological concept – that of *class composition* – which will help to clarify much of my further argument. By class composition I mean that combination of political and material characteristics, both historical and physical, that makes up (a) the historically given structure of labour power, in all its manifestations, as produced by a given level of productive forces and relations; and (b) the working class as a determinate level of solidification of needs and desires, as a dynamic subject, an antagonistic force tending towards its own independent identity, in historical–political terms. All concepts that define the working class must be framed in terms of this historical transformability of the composition of the class. This is to be understood in the general sense of its ever wider and more refined productive capacity, the ever greater abstraction and socialization of its nature, and the ever greater intensity and weight of the political challenge it presents to capital – in other words, *the remaking of the working class*! It is by reference to this framework and these criteria, for example, that we can qualify more precisely a term such as 'spontaneity'. The concept of composition allows us to introduce a specific, determinate quality into our theoretical definition of spontaneity; it prevents us, in other words, from falling into the trap of ideological definitions (whether political, in which case spontaneity is conceived of as an indifferent category, or economistic, in which case spontaneity is reduced to the semantic emptiness of the concept of labour power, plain and simple). The category of 'mass worker' must accordingly be reassessed, in its functions and limitations, within this temporal framework of the transformations of the composition of the working class. And, under today's conditions, it seems to me that this transformation is taking place through a process of real subsumption of labour by capital, a process that has now reached a level that encompasses the whole of society. *Hic Rhodus, hic salta* [Here is Rhodes, jump here!]

2   Capitalist restructuring: From the mass worker to social labour power

So let us return to the moment when the pressure of this new spontaneity (that is, the spontaneous – but, as in the paradox I have described, both structural and structured – forms of expression of the new class composition, i.e. of the mass worker) brings about a crisis in the means of capitalist control over the production and reproduction of commodities.

I would suggest that this moment can be located chronologically within the decade 1960–1970. In that period, strikes and struggles created an upheaval within the existing framework of development, inducing a major series of critical phenomena (crises of capitalist control), of which the following seem to be the most important:

(1) The mass worker set in motion a *mobility* within the labour market. The subversive characteristics of this mobility appear to consist in an uncontrollable increase in the speed of flow and turnover of demands, and at the same time in a rigid and homogeneous escalation of those demands. If we include in our definition of the mass worker the fact that the mass worker represents a certain qualitative solidification of abstract labour (which is another way of saying a high level of subjective awareness of abstract labour), then these mobility-related phenomena reveal simply the centripetal potential of abstract labour (towards averageness, mediety) in a framework of mass production in modern capitalism. And this might be consistent with development. But, instead, the forms and modes in which the mobility (subjectivity) of the mass worker expressed itself threw capitalist development out of proportion, subjected it to intolerable accelerations, and in particular confronted it with the quality of this very composition – those historical differences and divisions of sex, age, culture, and so on that were now tending towards a deeply rooted political homogeneity. *Mobility of abstract labour equals tendency for subjects and for struggles to unify.*

(2) On the other hand, in a complementary process, the mass worker set in motion, both in individual factories and in the productive fabric of the metropolis, a *downward rigidity* of expectations and wage demands. This in itself (the demand for 'parity') became a subversive force. Drives towards egalitarianism served to reinforce this rigidity: we saw the collapse of all – or virtually all – the weaponry of division in the factory (piecework, employers' unilateral control of timings of the labour process, internal mobility, etc.) and of the hierarchy that controls the labour process and the organization of production. In this period, sackings – together with all the other various forms of exclusion and marginalization – were powerfully contested, resisted, and in large part blocked. Furthermore, the overall rigidity of the class brought about a reduction in effective labour time; it also provided defence and backup for individual experiences of resistance to work or refusal of work. The wage struggle, in both its qualitative and

quantitative aspects, became a powerful independent variable of development: a kind of economic–political dual power that came into existence. (In some instances we find this registered in factory legislation – most notably in Italy, for example.) *Rigidity of abstract labour equals qualitative consolidation of the previously mentioned unification of subjects and of struggles.*

(3) Third, the social mobility and the political and wage rigidity of the social worker were also articulated within the sphere of *circulation*. But, for the mass worker, circulation means a radical change in the relation between daily work time and non-work time. We were not yet at the point where the latter had hegemony over the former. However, this was a phase in which the social relation of production (the relation between production and reproduction) was an area of powerful contestation. Without succeeding in fully controlling and carrying through this leap in the class struggle, mass workers nevertheless spread the infection of their subjective behaviour into the fabric of proletarian society. First – just to take one example – although not yet at the point of directly contesting the 'Oedipal wage' (in other words, the wage paid for the male worker's domination over his family), the mass worker nonetheless induced an awareness of the urgent need for new wage forms in the management and development of the social sphere – new wage forms likely to have a decisive and dissolving effect on the unified family wage and to liberate new labour power at an extremely high level of needs. The mass worker was an active factor in the circulation of working-class objectives and in propagating the equality implicit in abstract labour. As such, the mass worker induced subversive effects within society that tended to negate the division between productive and reproductive labour, and also to alter the established proportion between them. The circulation of the forms of behaviour of the mass worker was an extension of the unification of the subjects and of the struggles.

(4) Finally, I have to stress that it is only by moving to a *political* expression that the series of subversive conditions implicit in the existence of the mass worker could be further advanced. The concept of the mass worker had an existence that was purely relative; the fact that mass workers were the point of a class evolution that had not yet been fully realized often permitted the surreptitious reintroduction of old political concepts and practices, such as the notion of vanguard and mass, and thus permitted the re-emergence of party representation and the mirroring of past

forms. This political inadequacy results from precisely the social indeterminateness of the figure of the mass worker. We should never underestimate this limitation but, if we look beyond it, we can see that a *framework of new values* was beginning to take shape – ideas of freedom to match the fact of mobility; ideas of community, as an aspect of the rigidity mentioned; ideas of new life and universality, as a synthesis of people's relation to reproduction and liberated time. This framework of new values was incipient, was still dawning, but was nonetheless efficacious, because it existed at a mass level.

At this point the capitalist crisis in the management of *this* labour power, with all its strength and richness, became decisive. Capital goes into crisis every time labour power transmutes to become working class – and by 'working class' I mean a level of composition incompatible with command, at a given historical level of maturity of the productive forces. (It is evident that consciousness cannot be defined outside this relation; so it is possible to find extremely high levels of consciousness that remain totally ineffective and, on the other hand, spontaneous levels of consciousness that are powerfully effective in revolutionary terms.) As I say, every time when labour power effects a revolutionary transformation in its composition and becomes working class, at that point capital enters relations of crisis and has only one weapon with which to respond: *restructuring* – an attempt to attack and transform class composition. In other words, for capital, restructuring is a political, economic and technological mechanism aimed at the enforced reduction of the working class to labour power. To put it more correctly, capital aims to reduce the intensity of the political composition of the class.

At this point, the problem becomes specific again. How did capital respond to the crisis in relations of production that was induced by the class offensive of the mass worker? How was restructuring articulated at this level of political composition of the class and its struggles? What happened after the 1960s?

It is not hard to identify and describe some major elements of the capitalist response. Obviously, the notes that follow are very partial and indicative. They limit themselves to questions of class relations in the sphere of production. To deal adequately with the restructuring of labour power, I would really have to consider two fundamental shifts in imperialist development in the early 1970s: the freeing of the dollar from gold parity (1971) and the energy crisis of 1973–74. There is no space to deal with them here, and so the argument, as well as being partial and indicative, is frankly insufficient. However, I would ask you to trust the author and believe me when I say that I have given a lot of thought to these other fundamental determinations of the overall framework. These, in my opinion, are not contradictory with the phenomena that are now studied at the level of production and reproduction. Rather they present an overdetermination, an extension and a deepening of the logic which lies at the root of these phenomena.

So let's return to my initial question, to the analysis of the groundwork of capitalist restructuring. Let's begin by looking at *mobility*. In my opinion, as regards mobility, capital was already taking into account developments in the composition of the mass worker and was in fact acting on their tendency to become realized, in order to throw the working class back to the position of being labour power. While the composition of the mass worker from the 1960s onwards tended, via mobility, towards a unification in general of potential abstract labour, capital's restructuring project effectively grasps the social tendency towards abstract labour. It is against this abstract labour that capital exercises its capacity to repress, to fragment and to introduce hierarchical division. Capital does not mobilize against abstract labour and the social dimension it assumes, but against the political unification that takes place at this level. Capital assumes subsumption of labour (abstraction and socialization) as a process that has been realized. Experiments in job design, segmentation of the labour market, policies of regrading, reforms of methodologies of command within production cooperation, and so on – all this became fundamental. A restless, practical process of trial and error was now set in motion, aimed at destroying any possibility of proletarian unification. If we understand mobility as a tendency towards freedom, as a definition of time that is alternative to commanded time within the classic working day – and if we assume that from now on, in a parallel movement, it becomes impossible for capital to establish any fixed 'reserve army' of labour – then we understand why, in political and economic terms, it is so urgent for capital somehow to *fix* this labour power (the first, spontaneous and structural manifestation of an abstract labour that has become subjectively realized) within mobility and via mobility. We have on the one hand class struggles within and against capital's system and, on the other, capital struggles within and against the new composition: within its mobility, its socialization, its abstraction, and against the subjective attitudes which these elements engender. All manpower and job design interventions are to be understood as policies that learn from the progress of abstract labour towards its social unification: they intervene in order to block further development of its subversive potential.

Capital's reaction against the rigidity evident in the composition of the mass worker was even more rigorous. This is because in this area mystification is harder to achieve. Policies aimed at segmenting the labour market (which are posited as 'positive', as against the 'negative' of mobility of abstract labour) tend to produce a balkanization of the labour market and, above all, important new effects of marginalization: marginalization in the form of political blackmail, repression and degeneration of values – much more than the familiar blackmail of poverty. I have said that the rigidity in the forms of behaviour of the mass worker (particularly on the wages front) expressed an essence that was qualitative – a complex of needs that became consolidated as power. Capital's problem was how to defuse this power, quantitatively and qualitatively.

Thus, on the one hand, we have seen the promotion of various forms of *diffuse labour* –the conscious shifting of productive functions not tied to extremely high degrees of organic composition of capital towards the peripheries of metropolitan areas: this is the quantitative response, of scale and size. (The scale of this project is multinational and should be understood against the backdrop of the energy crisis.) On the other hand, capital has attacked the problem of qualitative rigidity and has planned for one of two solutions: it must be either corporatized or ghettoized. This means on the one hand a system of wage hierarchies, based on either simulated *participation* in development or *regimentation* within development, and on the other hand marginalization and isolation. On this terrain – a terrain that the experience of the struggles of the mass workers had revealed as strongly characterized by political values – capitalism's action of restructuring has often made direct use of legal instruments. It has regarded the boundary between legality and extralegality in working-class behaviours as a question subordinate to the overall restoration of social hierarchy. Not even this is new – as we know, it has always been the case – and Marx, in his analysis of the working day, makes the point several times. Law and the regulation of the working day are linked by a substantial umbilical cord. If the organization of the working day is socially diffuse, then sanctions, penalties, fines and so on will be entrusted to the competence of penal law.

Capital also acted against the way in which the mass worker *had made use of circulation* – in other words, of the increasingly tight links between production and reproduction. Restructuring once again adopted the method of displacement: capital takes as given or realized the tendency set in motion by working-class struggles, it subsumes its behaviours (i.e. the awareness of the circularity between production time and reproduction time) and begins working on how to control this situation. The welfare state is the principal level geared to synchronizing this relationship. The benefits of the welfare state are the fruit of struggles, the counterpower. But the specific application of restructuring aims to use welfare in order to control, to articulate command via budgetary manoeuvrings. 'Public spending cuts' are not a negation of the welfare state; rather they reorganize it in terms of productivity and repression. If subsequently proletarian action within this network of control continues to produce breakdown and to introduce blockages and disproportions, then capital's insistence on control reaches fever pitch. The transition to the internal warfare state represents the corresponding overdetermination of the crisis of the welfare state. But it is important to stress once again capital's capacity for displacement. The restructuring that has followed the impact of the mass worker's struggles and the tendencies that the mass worker has instilled within the general framework of class power relations are geared to match a labour power that exists as completely socialized – whether it exists or potentially exists is not important. Capital is forced into anticipation. However, marginalization is as far as capital can go in excluding people from the circuits of production; expulsion is impossible. Isolation within the circuit of production – this is the most that capital's action of restructuring can hope to achieve. It does not succeed in bringing about a restoration of the status quo, and in the struggle against the mass worker it is likely to assist in the even more compact formation of a completely socialized labour power. There is much craftiness of proletarian reasoning in all this!

Things become even clearer when we come to the fourth area in which capital's activity of restructuring has to prove itself and be proven: the terrain of *politics*. Here every attempt at mystification – this seems to me the most interesting aspect – is forced to assume the complete socialization of labour power as normal, as a fact of life, a necessary precondition of any action against proletarian antagonism. In other words, as many writers now accept, the only, remote possibility of mystifying (controlling, commanding etc.) struggles is conditional on an advancement of the terms in which the problem is considered: on an approach to the problem at the level of policies of capitalist command that see its enemy subject in proletarian society as a whole. Capital relates to the phase of real subsumption as antagonism at the highest level. Capitalist analyses of command move from this awareness to develop two possible lines of approach. The first, which I would call 'empirical', regards social labour power as a purely economic subject, and therefore locates the necessary, control-oriented manoeuvrings within a continuous trial-and-error process of redistribution and reallocation of income – for example consumerist objectives and inflationary measures. The other, which I call 'systemic', is more refined. It assumes that the empirical policies pursued thus far have resolved nothing. Thus the only way of ensuring the effective exercise of command, with an ongoing reduction of the complexity of class conflict, is to maintain command over systemic information and circulation, to maintain a pre-ordered mechanism of planning and balancing inputs and outputs. At this level, capital's science and practice of command reveal themselves as a set of techniques for analysing the social sphere – and as an undoubtedly involuntary recognition of the immediate sociality, structure and density of labour power.

I consider it important to understand these fundamental changes and to highlight their conceptual character. Thus I define restructuring as a parenthesis within the evolving process of the composition of the working class. Obviously, this is a necessary parenthesis: the interaction of productive forces (capital and the working class) is in no sense illusory. But at the same time I should stress that, within this process, the motor force of working-class struggles is fundamental, as are the intensity of their composition and the emergence of abstract labour as a social quality and as a unifying factor within production (and reproduction). As we used to say, capital's great function is to create the conditions for its own destruction. This is still the case. Thus we must recognize that, in the restructuring process currently under way, these critical conditions of capitalist development are still respected. Obviously, such a recognition is possible only if our theory is up to it. And one of the fundamentals of an adequate theory is to have a concept of labour power that is not conceptually indiscriminate but that is historically and politically pregnant, is continually and materially in tune with class consciousness – in other words, with degrees of struggle and of capacity to effect change that come increasingly close to the classic concept of proletariat. However, I feel that it is still necessary to live through that ambiguity of production and relations of production, and the way they are always being newly determined.

3   Towards a critique of the political economy of the mass worker: From social labour power to the social worker

So our project is to resolve this fundamental ambiguity in the relationship that labour power (whether posited as individual commodity or as socialized abstract labour) has with class consciousness and with capital. In other words, at this point we have to ask ourselves whether the *linear* mechanism of Marx's analysis, which locates the socialization and the abstraction of labour within the process of real subsumption of labour under capital, is not perhaps incorrect. The process of real subsumption, in Marx, concludes in a real and proper *Aufhebung*: the antagonism is transcended via an image of communism that is the necessary outcome of the dialectical process developed up to that point. In the more banal of the socialist vulgates, the *Aufhebung* – whose schema, in Marx, is conceptual, structural and synchronic – becomes diachronic, utopian and eschatological. To further clarify this point, I shall spell out my thesis: *at the level of real subsumption* (i.e. at the level of the complete socialization and abstraction of all the productive and reproductive segments of labour), *we are dealing not with linearity and catastrophe, but with separation and antagonism.* It seems to me that proof of this theory is to be sought first and foremost from empirical analysis (historical, sociological and political) of the movements of the working class, in other words from considering the characteristics of labour power when posited as social labour power.

Concretely, our argument could proceed from the examination of a familiar historical conjuncture: if, as some authors have done, we construct historical charts that map developments in the quality of work, then we can see how the entire direction of capitalist development is towards the destruction of skilled labour (of specific 'skill'), reducing it to abstract labour (the multilateral 'job'). The socialization of educational processes (schooling, skill training, apprenticeships) goes hand in hand with the process of the abstraction of labour, within a historical series of episodes that span the entire period since the Industrial Revolution. Within this time span, the tendency is progressive and broadly balanced, beginning from the eighteenth century and moving through to the 1920s–1930s: *but at this point a break takes place in the balanced continuity of the historical series.* The collapse of 'skilled work' can be located precisely in the period between the two big imperialist wars

– that is, in the 1920s and 1930s. This resulted in the hegemony, as from that period, of the semi-skilled worker, the *ouvrier spécialisé* (OS) – what we call the mass worker. But it also turns out that this hegemony is transitory because the mass worker is in fact just *the first* figure in the collapse of the balanced relationship between 'skill' and 'job'; the mass worker is *the first* moment of an extraordinary acceleration towards a complete abstraction of labour power. The *mass worker, the semi-skilled worker* (whatever his subjective consciousness) *is not so much the final figure of the skilled worker, but rather the first impetuous prefiguration of the completely socialized worker.*

This premiss has a number of important consequences. Without losing myself in casuistry, it is worth highlighting just one consequence, which seems fundamental in characterizing a critique of the political economy of the mass worker. It runs as follows: if 'skill' collapses into an indifferent element; if the division of labour as we know it (based on vertical scales of relative intensity and of structural quality) dissolves; if every theory of 'human capital' (i.e. of the self investment of labour power) reveals itself to be not only a mystification of a reality that is exploited and subjected to command but also pure and simple fantasizing apologetics; if, as I say, all this is given, it does nothing to remove the fact that capital still needs to exercise command by having and maintaining a differentiated and functional structuring of labour power to match the requirements of the labour process (whether this be individual or social).

In the previous section I noted some of the basic characteristics of capitalist restructuring in the transition from the mass worker to socialized labour power. We can grasp the theoretical kernel of the matter by returning to them for a moment. As I said, once there is a lapse of such vertical differentiations as between 'skill' and 'job', collective capital (and state command) tend to advance new differentiations, on the horizontal terrain of command, over the labour market, over the social mobility of labour power. In relation to advanced capitalism, this is familiar territory: it is the terrain of *new industrial feudalism* (what we would call 'corporatism'). From within this particular balance of forces, there proliferate a host of theories about the division of labour power: the debate as to whether labour power is primary, secondary or tertiary; whether it is 'central' or 'peripheral'; and so on. What is the substance of the problem? Social labour power is understood as mobility, and it is as such that it is to be regulated. (A short aside: in this regard, all static theories about industrial reserve armies and similar nineteenth-century archaeological constructs, as well as needing to be politically rejected by us, are obviously logically untenable.)

But let me be more precise about what I mean when I say that social labour power is understood as mobility. I mean that labour power is understood as social, mobile and subjectively capable of identity. I mean that capital understands as a present reality what, for the mass workers weighed down by the contradictions implicit in their own social gestation, was present purely as tendency. And above all I mean a substantial modification in the level at which we consider the problem.

Mobility is time, flow and circulation within time. Marxism bases its categories on the *time measure of the working day.* In certain well-known Marxist texts, the convention of time measure becomes so solid and unquestioned as to postulate as its base a working day that is 'normal'. Now, in our present situation, of all this there remains no trace. The time of social labour power is a working day so extended as not only to comprise within itself the relation between production time and reproduction time, as a single whole, but above all to extend the consideration of time over the entire life space of the labour market. From the working day to the labour market, from working hours to the mobility of labour, this transition means counterposing two opposing conceptions of time: the capitalist conception of time measure and the conception of working-class freedom over the temporal span of life. The capitalist operation of reducing lifetime to an abstract labour time measure becomes an operation that is absolutely antagonistic. In its conception of time and development, it reveals a substantial dissymmetry with proletarian life, with the very existence of social labour power. Here we can say that the dissymmetry of command in general (the dissymmetry revealed by theories of the state), and in particular the dissymmetry that regulates the categories of exploitation, become dislocated and reshaped in the face of the long social time of proletarian existence.

In arguing my case, I want to stress this point. The reason is clear. If it is true that the terms of exploitation are now relocated on the social terrain and if, within this social terrain, it is no longer possible to reduce quantity and quality of exploitation, absolute surplus value and relative surplus value, to the time measure of a 'normal' working day – then the proletarian subject is reborn in antagonistic terms, around a radical alternative, an alternative of life time as against the time measure of capital. But, even if we limit our arguments to a critique of the political economy of the mass worker, we are still able to achieve positive results on this question – namely that the ambiguous concept of the mass worker here reveals its structural indeterminacy and instability: its ambiguity is that between a system of domination still internalized by the mass worker (capital's time measure) and a perspective on work that is calculated and envisaged over the time of an entire life. Mass workers are still prey to ideology – their memory is of slavery, while their actions speak of freedom. Capitalist restructuring, which anticipates and outmanoeuvres the struggles of the mass worker by introducing the dimension of social labour power, at this point arrives at a definitive contradiction, inasmuch as any transcendence of the mass worker has to be, not a reproduction and reformulation of domination over socialized labour power, but a resolution of the contradictory tensions within the figure of the mass worker and the structural realization of the antagonism in a new form.

The social worker: let us define the way the antagonism has become subjectivized at this level, and call socialized labour power 'the social worker'. In this way we are clearly introducing a specific methodological difference – in any event a position that differs from those developed in earlier phases of the theory of the mass worker and in the methodology that was considered adequate for the maturation of that theory. The specificity and the difference lie in the quality of the antagonism that appears at this point. In other words this abstract, social and mobile labour power – to the extent that it subjectivizes itself around its own concept of time and a temporal constitution of its own (which are irreducible to the time measurement of capitalist command) – brings about an *irreducible antagonism*: irreducible not only to labour power, conceived of as variable capital, and to the theoretical dialectic of value, all of which is perfectly obvious, but above all irreducible to the far more refined dialectic of composition, restructuring and recomposition that, from a class point of view, had been developed as a portrayal integral to the historical experience of the mass worker. In reality this portrayal, in its further versions, maintained a concept of the working day that was modelled on the capitalist conception of a time measure. But when the whole of life becomes production, capitalist time measures only that which it directly commands. And socialized labour power tends to unloose itself from command, insofar as it proposes a life alternative – and thus projects a different time for its own existence, both in the present and in the future. When all life time becomes production time, who measures whom? *The two conceptions of time and life* come into direct conflict, in a separation that becomes increasingly deep and rigidly structured. But we shall come to all this in the next section.

Let's now return to our critique of the political economy of the mass worker. At the cost of repeating myself, I must stress once again both the importance and the ambiguity of that category. Its importance lies in the fact that, with the historical emergence of the mass worker, the concept of labour power removes itself definitively from the theory-imposed destiny of being a component – albeit variable – of capital. But in the act of revealing itself as an *independent variable* (and clashing with a capitalist restructuring that relentlessly tracks, adjusts and recomposes the struggles), the constitutive activity of the mass worker, even though moving in a situation of complete socialization of production, failed to reach a sufficient degree of maturity. This brought about powerful ambiguities, and also, in the 1970s, a degree of political retrogression: a corporatism of certain strata of the mass worker, new divisions within the class, and so on. But this is the point where the character of the *social worker* emerges as a new force and as a subjective qualification of social labour power. The social worker completed and concluded the dynamic that existed within the mass worker as a tendency, and transformed the independent variable into independence *tout court*. This antagonism develops at a pace dictated by the rhythms of the real subsumption, which capital puts into operation in relation to social labour. As real subsumption advances, so the social worker is brought into existence, as irresolvable antagonism: antagonism as regards conceptions of life, the liberation of time, and thus in bringing about spatial–temporal conditions that are wholly alternative. It is a sort of a priori of liberation.

But before I resume this line of argument, allow me to point out an apparent paradox in the theory – which in this case turns out to be a function of mystification. In the so-called postmodern (or post-capitalist) conceptions that are so current in political debate today, the process of subsumption is represented in terms of linearity and catastrophe. In some instances, these terms can also be found in Marx – and, in far more developed form and sometimes completely explicitly, in the socialist vulgate. Subsumption is given as a system, as labour power realized within capital's social domination, as a levelling-off of the antagonism – and therefore the antagonism is conceived of as a utopian and catastrophist alternative. Such positions are fairly widespread and sometimes also include exponents of the mass worker theory. In these workerist theories that are flirting with theories of postmodernism (stressing tendency and objectivity and eliminating antagonism and subjectivity), some would say that workerism is committing hara-kiri. The paradox and, at the same time, the mystification consist in the fact that here Marx's thinking (with the considerable tensions that run through it right up to the point where he defines real subsumption – whether in the unpublished Chapter VI or, a good while previously, in the 'Fragment on Machines' in the *Grundrisse*, texts that must be seen as complementary) *appears* to be respected, whereas in fact it is deeply and irreparably misrepresented. In fact the focus in Marx is always the actuality and the determinacy of the antagonism. It is indeed true that the theoretical tendency of capital, which Marx also describes (but only episodically, and, as I have said, in terms rather subordinated to the antagonistic spirit of his overall argument), on occasion accepts this criticism and fights shy of the more banal mystifications. Nevertheless, when pushed to the limit, the most we can get from this conception of antagonism is to see it in an *exogenous form:* catastrophe. But our task, in going beyond Marx, is to grasp the antagonism in its *endogenous form*, also at the level of real subsumption.

By this I mean that real subsumption of labour is a form of the crisis of capital. Understanding real subsumption of labour as crisis is one of the discoveries in store for communism as it goes 'beyond Marx'.

But this is not enough. In our rejection of postmodern ideologies (without, of course, denying their analytical efficacity), we also retrieve another element of the theoretical history of our Italian movement since the 1960s. Namely, while the ambiguous theory and methodology of the mass worker implied a dialectic of value that today the social worker rejects, there was also articulated therein an inherent practical activity of subversion, a self-valorizing independence (autonomy), which now the social worker lives as his own dignity and essence. Massimo Cacciari, the philosopher of *Krisis*, cries that, where there is crisis, there is no dialectic. Crisis would not be a form of the dialectic, or rather could be dialecticized only in the form of an *Aufhebung* – its own transcendence.[1]

No, replies the social worker, here there can be no *Aufhebung*, because here the confrontation is between *subjects that are different*. In moving from formal subsumption to real subsumption, capital overcomes obstacles, lives the continual reduction of the working class to labour power in terms of a continuous, long-term and progressive socialization of labour – in terms of a transition between class compositions at increasingly high levels of intensity and potential. *Once subsumption is completely realized, the only possible development is a transition from socialized labour power to the social worker, to the new class subject.* The tradition and theory of the mass worker can still be of help in stimulating us towards this new definition.

4   A political conception of labour power: The proletariat: Some problems

Having reached this point, we can now attempt a summary of some basic methodological assumptions that should help us to reach a partial conclusion and to pose new problems.

To start with, I regard as logically untenable any theory of labour power as a logical construct: an ambiguous and volatile essence, caught in a dichotomy between a tendency to become variable capital (the variable part of organic capital) and a tendency to become working class (i.e. a receptacle for consciousness that derives from the outside, the substance of a new Aristotelian *sunolon* [whole]). This instrumental and pure logic definition of labour power, which is both abstract and open to manipulation, has, historically speaking, been progressively negated (if I may simplify) through at least three concomitant processes.

- The first process is *the advance in the organic composition of capital* – which, as it internalizes massively labour power's relation to the structure of capital, at the same time eliminates from it all measure of proportionality in the relationship between the work done by the individual worker and the level of productivity achieved. Labour power as presented within the labour market as a multiplicity of individual labour powers can now be conceived of only as a totally marginal phenomenon.
- The second process, which takes the development of the organic composition of capital beyond the scope of the single firm and goes beyond its phenomenological appearance to see it as the *realization of the subsumption of social labour under collective capital*, has shown labour power to be a social entity. That which is marginalized as an individual becomes transformed, at the social level, into mobility, into an equivalence of abstract labour, into a global potentiality that has in it that generalized social knowledge that is now an essential condition of production.
- The third process, concomitant with those of individual marginalization and collective socialization, has brought about a conjunction between (a) the refusal of labour power to make itself available as a commodity (I see this as the effect of individual marginalization and of the collapse of any relationship between 'job' and 'skill') and (b) the socialization of this mode of class behaviour. I designate this as a 'third' process and consider it both innovative

and conceptually very rich, since *the coming together of individual marginalization and collective socialization* is no simple process of addition. Rather it is a historical process, which combines material elements and becomes at the same time *subjectivized* – in the sense that historical experience becomes transformed into irreversible qualities, into a second nature. Through the genesis of this process, *new subjective forces make their appearance.*

As a result of these processes, it should now be clear that labour power, at this level of subsumption of social labour by capital, so far from presenting itself as an intermediate entity, suspended between being a function of variable capital and becoming working class, now presents itself as a *social subject:* a subject that has internalized at the social level its refusal to be a commodity.

At the political and social level, this subject presents a complete materialization of consciousness within the structures of its own existence. Class consciousness, in other words, comes neither from the outside nor from afar: it must be seen as completely internal to a fact, a thing of class composition. The concept of class composition, which was developed originally through the analysis of the mass worker – as a means of classifying changes in the nature of labour power and as a critique of purely logical and economistic characterizations of these changes – can now be updated as a historico-political, subjective social definition of labour power. In view of this, we can appreciate the importance of the theoretical current that developed through the analysis of the mass worker, and above all we can appreciate how the specific antagonistic subjectivity of this class protagonist contributed, through its struggles, to going beyond and overcoming the limitations of the original theoretical conception. It seems to me that the mythical term 'proletariat' has been given a historical dimension and has become founded as a specific material reality through the development of this theoretical approach.

Major consequences derive from all this. First, there is a *demystification* of a number of concepts and practices existing within the traditions of the labour movement. Secondly, in my opinion, important consequences (and, more particularly, problems) arise at the strictly theoretical level, in other words relating to our conceptions of work and communism. Thirdly, not to be underestimated in their importance, we also find indications of method.

Let us take the first point. This social labour power that exists as a political reality, this social worker, this proletariat, embraces within itself so many dimensions, both intensive and extensive, as to render many categories *obsolete*. In other words, proletarian antagonism (within real subsumption) posits itself on the one hand, intensively, as an irreversibility of the given level of needs that has been arrived at, and on the other hand, extensively, as a potentiality of action, as a capacity to extend action across the entire span of the working day. If we want a tighter conceptual definition, we might say that this social-ized labour power not only (a) dissolves any possibility for capitalism to consider it as a commodity, as the variable component of capitalist command for exploitation, but also (b) denies capitalism any pos-sibility of transforming necessary labour into wage and surplus value (absolute or relative) into profit. Clearly profit and wage continue to exist, but they exist only as quantities regulated by a relation of power – a relation of forces that no longer admits the threefold partition of the working day into necessary labour time, surplus labour time, and free time or reproduction time. We now have a labour power that is both social and subjective, that recognizes the value partition of the working day only as a system of command, which capital may or may not succeed in imposing over and against the continuous flow of labour power within the working day. *The conditions for the extrac-tion of surplus value now exist only in the form of a general social relation.* Profit and the wage become forms of the division of a value content that no longer relates to any specific mechanisms of exploitation other than the specific asymmetry of the relationship of command within society. Capital has the form and substance of profit, as an average, a mediety of command; labour power has the form and the substance of the wage, but in no way can a 'natural rate' be said to exist between the two of them. In other words, the mechanism of transformation and mediation that characterizes the Marxian gen-esis of these concepts has now reached its point of fullest maturity. Exploitation consists in command. It is violence against the antago-nism of social subjects that are fighting for liberation.

As a consequence, the marketing of labour power is no longer an undertaking for minions and sycophants: if anything, the market-ing of labour power today has become a totally political operation. This consists in extending Marx's 'war' between capitalism's ten-dency towards the limitless working day and the tendency of the proletariat to limit (to nil, if possible) the provision of labour power, and in transforming that 'war' into formalized and viable political procedures, which extend from the concrete labour process (within production and reproduction) to the overall scenario of the organi-zation of command – that is, to political and state forms of the management of the economy, management of the labour market, of public spending, and so on. Only in this political dimension can success or failure in the marketing of labour power now be gauged.

All of this is another way of saying that, at our given level of development, the old dialectic of labour power [*la dialettica della forza lavoro*] within and against capital is now played out, has become obsolete, is only of archaeological interest. If there exists any real negotiation or bargaining, this can no longer be encompassed by trade union forms of bargaining or other such antique practices. In other words, *the dualism of power is now the norm*. The working day can be described only in terms of an active dualism of power wherein the old dialectic of unity, transcendence and equilibrium is obsolete. In making this point I need only refer, by way of example, to the inadequacy of the most normal, everyday and (as it often seems) obvious institutional form of the traditional labour movement: the trade union.

Far more dangerous, as regards the potential mystification of our own concept, rediscovered and reconstructed, of the proletariat, are those ideologies that take labour power as a material that can be led to class consciousness (although they are also more ineffective, given the historical experience of 'realized socialism' in the east). To turn labour power into what? To transmute exploited labour into liberated labour, via the magic wand of a mystical 'political consciousness', in other words of its vanguard representatives. What has changed in reality? Nothing – only words. The dialectic of labour functions here perfectly. The word 'labour' replaces the word 'capital': the system remains the same. The working day is not touched. Time measure continues to be the regulative function of command and of partition or division. No – the new (and even the old?) concept of the proletariat really cannot accept these mystifications. The truth is that, from the proletarian point of view, the process of real subsumption brings about such a massive intensification of the composition of the working class, and such an extension of its potentiality, as to eliminate any dualism between being and consciousness, any isolation of single aspects within it. The proletariat acts directly over the entire span of the social working day. Production and reproduction are now, in parallel and on equal terms, the spheres of action proper and adequate to the reality of labour power. Consciousness is an attribute, entirely within and of its material structure.

And now let's look at work, labour. Here we come to the second set of consequences deriving from our political concept of socialized labour power, of composition (i.e. of the social worker). Labour is the essence of capital. It always has been so. It is also the essence of the human being, inasmuch as the human being is productive activity. But capital is real – while human essence is only a dream. *The only human essence of labour that approximates to the concreteness of capital is the refusal of work* – or rather that kind of productivity that, for capital, is purely negative – because, while it represents a *sine qua non* of production, capital nonetheless tends to reduce it, and, precisely insofar as it is an essence of human nature, to eliminate it from production. Human labour, when posited as proletarian reality, is a negative element in capitalist production. Of course, it is true to say that only labour produces. But it is also true that bosses are happy with production only when the labour in it is totally under command: command is sadistic, it requires the presence of human labour, but only in order then to deny it, to nullify it. This process has functioned in the past as the classic steely scourge of capitalist domination – until and unless labour power presents itself as a social subject. In other words we have here, within the intensity and extensity of the composition of the proletarian subject, a negative form of labour, which has such broad dimensions and is so articulated as to render problematical its very definition as 'negative'. We often refer to it as 'alternative', 'self-valorizing' and so on. But I prefer to continue calling it 'negative labour', not in order to flirt with the language of crisis but simply because I do not yet feel the *strength* to be able to call it liberated work (i.e. work that is wholly positive). It is difficult to describe any work as 'positive' so long as it is contained within capital, such is the quantity of death and pain that it bears within it. For us to call working-class and proletarian work 'positive' and socially useful, we would have to be capable – the proletarian subject in its overall complexity would have to be capable – of the statement in prefigurative terms of its alternative form of production. We would require a vision of how its own productive potential could unfold. (Only certain sectors of the proletariat within the area of reproduction – the feminist movement chief among them – have so far proved capable of producing a positive image of forms of work that could be proletarian, alternative and revolutionary.) But the fact that we cannot spell it out does not necessarily mean that it does not exist. It exists as a murmuring among the proletariat. Negative work, amid the whispers of everyday life and the noise and shouting of the struggle, is beginning to gain a general form of expression. What I think needs stressing particularly is the *material character* of negative work, *its institutionality*. The concept of proletariat is becoming an institutional reality, a practical emergence – not lifeless, but living; a different conception of time; a universality held within that second nature, entirely factitious (in etymological terms, *verum ipsum factum*); an institutionality, thus, that seeks order and a systematization of its own values. The levels, the spaces of this experience are truly thousand-fold. But they all have a centripetal impulse, which increases according to the extent of their liberty, their expansivity. If we are to translate the word 'communism' into present-day language, then perhaps it means reinforcing and solidifying this proletarian institutionality and developing its potential contents.

However, for the moment we still require a long period of clarification, of study, and of specific struggles. The method remains tactical. *Methodological consequences* derive from our definition of the proletarian subject as antagonism within realized subsumption – and they derive, above all, from our understanding of the various aspects of the transition from mass worker to socialized labour power, to the social worker. Within this transition, simultaneously with the breakdown of the regulatory principles of capitalist development (the market, value, the division between production and reproduction etc.), there also unfolds the impossibility of any homogeneous and unified determination not only of the overall design of development, but particularly of its categories, its norms. When the concept of labour power is realized within a socialized and subjectified class composition – and this takes place precisely at the highest point of unity from capital's viewpoint (real subsumption) – then all the established terms of scientific argument break down. They become blocked, definitively non-recuperable for the old dialectical logic of unity and transcendence. The only way in which any scientific category, whether in logic or in ethics, in politics or in political economy, can constitute itself as a norm is as a *negotiated settlement*: as a formalization and balancing of opposing forces – in the human sciences, as a moment of voluntary agreement. It is clear that nothing of what defined the old conception of scientific norms is present here. What we have instead, exclusively, is the logical results brought about by the development of class composition – *subsumption under capital realized in the form of permanent crisis*. What we are presented with is the positive emergence of negative labour as an institutionalized counterpower, acting against work that is subsumed within capital. While labour subsumed under capital corresponded to a logic of unity, of command, and of its transcendence, *negative labour produces instead a logic based on separateness* – a logic that operates entirely within, is endogenous to, that separateness. The institutionalized forms now assumed by labour power as a *separate* entity also represent its deinstitutionalization in relation to the present framework of economy and politics, to capital and the state. This relation is precisely a negative one and, inasmuch as negative labour has the power and possibility of imposing it on the system, the only unifying logic that remains is one of duality, two-sidedness: a logic that is ephemeral, reduced to mere semblance. In reality it can represent only a moment in a historical phase of crisis, in which the point of reference for all rationality or intelligibility is being rapidly shifted towards a fully socialized labour power, the new class subject, the 'social worker'.

So I have covered, in outline, some aspects of the formation of labour power into a social subject. A very rich phenomenology could be provided for this transformation, starting from the mass worker and the history of the mass worker's struggles. I think that such an account would confirm the theoretical and methodological assumptions I have outlined here.

In conclusion, however, I would stress that, so far, this is only a half-way stage in the analysis. For, if it is true that every scientific category concerning the relation of capital can now be understood only within a *dualistic matrix*, then a further logical problem arises: the question of the multiplicity and mobility of the forms of this transformation of the class subject, and how this multiformity can be grasped *within* a mature political concept of labour power – in other words, how we can develop a theory of the new institutionality of the proletariat in its multiple matrices. But this will have to wait for another occasion.

2

On Recent Trends in the Communist Theory of the State⋆

A Critical Review

1 The revisionist tradition and the conception of the state

State monopoly capitalism (stamocap) consists in the subordination of the state apparatus to capitalist monopolies. Ever since Stalin fixed this definition for the Third International in the 1930s (thereby avoiding the tasks of analysis and modification of the political line of international communism that would have been required by the changes in progress in the capitalist state during the Great Depression),[1] the official wing of the workers' movement has advanced very little in exploring state theory. The mechanical and instrumental conception of the relationship between monopoly capital and the structure of the state has remained intact. Large-scale monopoly capital (a necessary excrescence of capitalist development) claims control over the movements of the state, continuously and point by point. The state comes to merge with large-scale monopoly capital (as a specific and limited part of global capital [*capitale complessivo*]) and is subordinate to it.[2] The eventual modification of juridical structures, be they managerial or proletarian, of large-scale monopoly capital does not affect the subordination of the state; rather it accentuates the interpenetration of ruling elites and reaffirms the nature and direction of monopoly command: 'In reality, what appear to be conflicts between business

⋆ Originally published in the journal *Critica del diritto* 3, 1974, pp. 84–120, under the title 'Su alcune tendenze della più recente teoria comunista dello Stato: Rassegna critica', then reproduced in Antonio Negri, *La forma stato*, Milan: Feltrinelli 1977, pp. 196–232.

and government are reflections of conflict within the ruling class.'[3] Neither is the instrumental relationship of subordination modified by the development of a supranational or multinational organization of the monopolies and of stamocap; indeed, if anything, it is accentuated.

The political aim of such a representation of the state (as the 'slave of the monopolies') is immediately understandable and familiar to anyone who is reasonably familiar with the politics of the official labour movement. This tradition involves organizing the broadest possible front against the outgrowths of capitalist development and the distortions induced by the power of monopolies; imposing, on behalf of the whole of society, a new model of development onto the state, which otherwise is the site of mediating the power of monopolies and of transmitting their will; fighting, through reforms that attack the monopolistic organization of the state, against the despotic character of its relation to society; and purging the state from the influence of the monopolies through the broadest possible system of social alliances. In short, this tradition involves opening an antagonistic dialectic between civil society and the state of monopoly capitalism (often also called 'fascist') in the name of democracy and the majority.

> The State is related to the monopoly fraction as its agent/tool: this relation is understood as a conspiracy which uses personal contacts to place the State (still, however, capable of conducting the revolution from above) in the hands of a small group of monopolists. Let the people as a whole drive out these usurpers and the State will do the rest![4]

So these are the political objectives of stamocap theory. It is clear that a different or opposite conception of the state will involve different and opposite tactics and strategies.

However, a number of objections arise within stamocap theory itself. Some people[5] have attempted to play down the declaration that a fusion has occurred between the state and the forces of monopoly: monopoly capitalism and the state are independent forces that converge, but there is no rigid and unilateral subordination of the state to the monopolies. Yet these objections do not carry much weight, insofar as they lack the power to problematize the relationship between state, capital, and society and thus to reassert the notion of the state as an independent social function. And even when, as in the best textbook available today,[6] there is clear awareness that we have entered into a new phase of the relations between state and capital, a phase that is 'qualitatively new' from the point of view of the interpenetration of the two horizons, this awareness does not translate into an analysis of the overall process of the social reproduction of capital, but works merely in particular areas (technology, science, and so on).

It seems that quite different problems arise from the current phase of the class struggle, from the theory that inhabits it and from the attempted strategies that emanate from it. The theory of stamocap seems oblivious to the quality of the relationship between capital and state, namely of the fact that their articulation develops at the level of the whole society, which is entirely absorbed by what is required for the reproduction of capital. From this point of view, stamocap theory can be seen as a variant of the theories of the state that concern themselves with elites and, caught up in the analysis of a specific state, forgets various substantive elements of the materiality of state organization – namely legality, 'its' justice, the claims to consensus, the continuity and efficacy of mediation mechanisms, and so on.[7] All these elements are relegated to the field of subjectivity, so that the implacable and obsessive image of big monopoly capital ends up moving on a singularly soggy and vacant terrain (which should also be the terrain on which antagonisms emerge). The capitalist economy of the state is a closed system, with objective validity and efficacy. This is in essence the basic belief of the theory, and its consequence is a purely instrumental conception of the state. Political activity is relegated to a sphere of merely subjective autonomy, and this leads to the banal adoption of democracy as a hypothesis for mobilizing oppressed civil society against the overweening power of monopoly.[8]

We need to examine a number of apparently contradictory features of stamocap theory. Its sheer opportunism is shown essentially in the ambiguity that is established between an objective aspect (the state–monopoly relationship as a mechanical and material nexus, of a necessary nature) and a subjective aspect (the state–politics relationship as an instrumental and voluntary nexus). The state is structure inasmuch as it is subordinated to monopoly; it is purely ideological superstructure insofar as it is a political state. The same applies to civil society, which on the one hand is subordinated to the repressive structure necessary for monopolistic development, and on the other is voluntaristically idealized as a possible site for conflict and antagonism. In fact the only truly antagonistic element in the process lies in the contradictions of monopolistic development itself. From this point of view, stamocap theory comes close to being a purely objectivist version of the theory of catastrophic collapse.

Anyone seeking to find the place of working-class struggle in stamocap theory will come away empty-handed. Actually the problem of a connection between the materiality of exploitation in the process of production and reproduction of capital and the structures of capitalist development (and crisis) is often not even raised. Or rather it is solved beforehand whenever the need for the process of capitalist reproduction in the form of state monopolism and the completely ideological character of class struggles are taken as givens. On the other hand, the only objective of class struggle is the re-establishment of the capitalist rationality of development ('socialism'?), as a counter to the deformations induced by the monopolistic order.[9] In the extreme and dominant conceptions of stamocap theory, the space of class struggle is a space of simply ideological intermediation, and thus becomes analogous to the space of democratic struggle. The struggle of the working class merges into and cancels itself in the struggle of the 'broad masses', discounting all its qualitative specificity. Any relationship between class goals and power goals falls by the wayside.

The less extreme versions of stamocap theory continue to be marked by a reductive conception of class struggle. In particular, in the most recent literature there are references to a socialization of the monopolistic articulation of power, as already mentioned. They point to the extension and compactness of the interrelationships between the monopolistic state and the techno-scientific structure of society.[10] Here the ambiguity is maximal, and the discrepancy between an 'objective factor' and a 'subjective factor' risks exploding. Nevertheless, even here, the presence of class struggle remains minimal. The contradiction is socialized only along revisionist lines reminiscent of Engels and with a technocratic flavour (the 'control room' [*la 'camera dei bottoni'*], the 'salami theory' of power, and so on), when it does not immediately short-circuit back to the dialectic of the objective contradictions of monopoly.

From a methodological point of view, stamocap theory is characterized by an extreme neutralization of categories and of Marxism and by an extremization of the fetishism of ideology, of the autonomy of ideology, and of the political will of the masses.[11] These apparently divergent but substantially concomitant tendencies add up to a distortion and mystification of unity from the class point of view. In short, stamocap theory is a theory that finds its logic in the dysfunctions of capitalist distribution and is totally incapable of reconnecting the institutional world of the social reproduction of capital to the working-class point of view, which moves from an understanding of, and from the fight against, exploitation.

Whatever the logic was that accounts for the genesis of the communist theory of state capitalism, and whatever the motives were that led to its renewal in the 1960s, it has to be said that this theory is now a rotten planet from which we need to distance ourselves as quickly as possible.[12]

2   Situating the problem: Marxian approaches

This long preamble on stamocap was necessary. As we shall see, despite the crudeness of stamocap's approach (or perhaps because of it), its resonance and direct influence are stronger than we might think. Besides, the consequences of this doctrine are enormous: it is not limited to a general definition of the monopoly relationship (the dominant capitalist economic reality) versus the state, but also implies a rather normative definition of the mechanism of the production of right (i.e. the norms of social action), a purely repressive, non-dialectical (short-, medium-, and long-term) conception of the relationship between the state and social conflictuality, and an attitude that is both cynical and adventurist ('pessimism of the intellect and optimism of the will') towards the relationship between state and class struggle. It is immediately obvious how sharply all this contrasts with the reality of the behaviour of the two struggling classes – capital and the working class. Yet stamocap justifies itself on the basis of a Marxist definition of the state. 'The executive of the modern State is but a committee for managing the common affairs of the whole bourgeoisie'; it is 'power organized in one class for the oppression of another'.[13] This is where the 'orthodoxy' of stamocap resides.

'Orthodoxy' is of no great interest. Yet, paying due homage to tradition, one could say (simplifying things as much as possible) that, alongside this definition of the state, there are at least two others in the work of Marx and Engels that are far more complex and intense.[14] One was already forming in *The German Ideology*:

> By the mere fact that it is a class and no longer an estate, the bourgeoisie is forced to organise itself no longer locally, but nationally, and to give a general form to its average interests. Through the emancipation of private property from the community, the state has become a separate entity, alongside and outside civil society; but it is nothing more than the form of organisation which the bourgeois are compelled to adopt, both for internal and external purposes, for the mutual guarantee of their property and interests. The independence of the state is only found nowadays in those countries where the estates have not yet completely developed into classes . . . where consequently no section of the population can achieve dominance over the others . . . Since the

state is the form in which the individuals of a ruling class assert their common interests, and in which the whole civil society of an epoch is epitomised, it follows that all common institutions are set up with the help of the state and are given a political form. Hence the illusion that law is based on the will, and indeed on the will divorced from its real basis – on free will.[15]

This definition finds its formulation determined between the *Grundrisse* and *Capital*: we are presented in this way with the 'concentration of bourgeois society in the form of the state'.[16] That is, the state gradually internalizes the mediation of capitalist interest in the reproduction of domination through the organization of society; the emancipation of the state from civil society is only the precondition for a subsequent dialectical and mediatory folding back onto and into civil society, within its conflictual fabric, in line with the rhythm of the class struggle. The mediation of the dialectic between a repressive and an organizational function becomes the figure, life and progress of the capitalist state.[17] From this point of view, the state is a chapter of *Capital* – 'the whole will be divided into six books: (1) On capital (containing several preliminary chapters); (2) On landed property; (3) On wage labour; (4) On the state; (5) International trade; (6) World market'[18] – and hence follows a dynamic of the state that is concomitant with that of capital: from the accumulation functions exercised by the state to the organization of credit and of the monetary system, from factory legislation to the organization of the working day.

A third moment, and a further definition of the state, is the following: the state intervenes at another crucial point in capitalist development, namely to maintain 'private production without the control of private property',[19] once the bourgeoisie has proved its 'incapacity for managing any longer modern productive forces'.[20] It is in this context that Engels introduces the figure of the state as the ideal collective capitalist: 'the more it proceeds to the takeover of productive forces, the more it actually becomes the national capitalist, and the greater the number of citizens whom it exploits'.[21] Engels's definition, which has a certain literary ring to it and has come into common usage, deserves closer examination:

> But the transformation, either into joint stock or into state ownership, does not do away with the capitalistic nature of the reproductive forces. In the joint stock companies this is obvious. And the modern state, again, is only the organization that capitalist society takes on in order to support the capitalist mode of production against the entrenchments as well of the workers as of *individual capitalists*.

In state-owned industries, then, 'the wage workers remain wage earn-
ers, proletarians. The capitalist relation is not done away with. It is
rather brought to a head.' In this sense the state, 'whatever its form,
is an essentially capitalist machine, a state of capitalists, the ideal collective capitalist'.[22]

Now, in seeking to restate the problem of capital's state in the light
of the definitions given above, we shall need to highlight a number of
elements that underpin Marx's discussion of the matter.

(a) The proposed definitions have a dynamic character in Marx
and correspond to different phases, or qualitative leaps, in the
relationship between state and capital and between the capitalist state and civil society. In both pairings, one moves between
minimal and a maximal integration – this is the path of Marx's
analytical project, insofar as it follows the real progression of
the tendency. So we move from a maximum in capital's instrumentalization of the state to a maximum in the capitalist state's
organizational integration of civil society. In the current phase of
the class struggle, the capitalist state displays a level of structural
integration of civil society that approaches the very high levels
predicted. The capitalist state begins to define itself in reality
as an 'ideal collective capitalist'; in some respects it comes to
identify its own defining categories with the defining categories
of 'productive capital'. If this is true, the fundamental problem
today is to study the structural materiality of the relationship
between the collective capitalist and the contemporary state;
it is to follow its organizational articulations, in other words
the nexuses of the social reproduction of capital, as they come
increasingly to be integrated and commanded by the state.
Contrary to what stamocap theory has done, what is required
is a structural theory of the state–capital–society relationship
and a political strategy matched to the structural nature of those
interrelations.

(b) The progressive dialectic of integration reveals a specific dynamic
of the overall mechanisms of exploitation – one that has a
direction, as schematically summarized at another point in
Grundrisse: 'Then the *state*. (State and bourgeois society. Taxes,
or the existence of the unproductive classes. – The state debt. –
Population. The state externally: colonies. External trade. Rate
of exchange. Money as international coin. – Finally the world
market. Encroachment of bourgeois society over the state. Crises.
Dissolution of the mode of production and form of society based

on exchange value. Real positing of individual labour as social and vice versa.'[23] In other words, the theory of the state has to be dialectically combined with the theory of the crisis of the capitalist mode of production, with the sensible theory that leads to the demolition of the historical barrier of labour. Hence the theory of the state must be linked to the theory of the working class dialectically, through the theory of the crisis. The analysis of the relation between state and the collective capitalist has, then, only a preparatory role for the specific analysis of the historical course of structural transformations and for the privileging of crisis as a fundamental moment of transformation.[24]

(c) Third, in line with the assumptions indicated so far, the structural analysis of the relationship between state and collective capital and the precise identification of changes during crisis have to be related to the analysis of class mechanisms (i.e. to the power relations in the struggle between the two classes), which preside over those transformations and give them meaning. Communist political strategy arises from the tendential unification – always restated at the different individual levels of the political composition of the working class – between the theory of state structure, crisis theory, and class theory. Any 'regional' analysis that refuses its own tendential reunification and refoundation on the basis of the established class practice risks being meaningless, if it is true that 'the real subject retains its autonomous existence outside the head just as before; namely as long as the head's conduct is merely speculative, merely theoretical. Hence, in the theoretical method, too, the subject, society, must always be kept in mind as the presupposition.'[25]

One should add that the most recent communist theory of the state touches broadly on the themes outlined here, in the order of their presentation. So it would make sense to organize the discussion around them, in the same order.

3   The current state of theory: The neo-Gramscian variant

But before addressing these issues directly, let me take a look at some versions of the most recent communist theory of the state. Although they accept, and indeed insist on, the need for a structural approach to the definition of the new quality of the state of capital, these versions seem incapable of connecting their analysis to the solid ground of the critique of political economy.

In the two most recent and most widely read studies – those of Ralph Miliband[26] and Nicos Poulantzas[27] – the intention and the line of attack are decidedly structuralist. In any case, a certain pragmatism in Miliband and an analytical intention formulated in Poulantzas orient their discussion towards elements of a new and material texture of the contemporary state. I can remark only in passing on the richness of the specific investigations pursued in both works. The problem is also correctly posed: one needs to define how and within what dimensions the 'relative autonomy' of the contemporary state is determined vis-à-vis the world of economic relations, while the class nature of the state remains intact. In short, one needs to analyse the dialectical articulations of the relationship between the contemporary state and the 'ideal collective capitalist'. But to what extent is the attempt successful?

In polemicizing with Miliband's work, Nicos Poulantzas[28] essentially directs at it two homogeneous and related lines of criticism. First, in point of methodology, Miliband has difficulties, according to him,

in comprehending social classes and the state as *objective structures*, and their relations as an *objective system of regular connections*, a structure and a system whose agents, 'men', are in the words of Marx, 'bearers' of it – *träger*. Miliband constantly gives the impression that for him social classes or 'groups' are in some way reducible to *inter-personal relations*, that the State is reducible to inter-personal relations of the members for the diverse 'groups' that constitute the State apparatus and finally that the relation between social classes and the state is itself reducible to inter-personal relations of 'individuals' comprising social groups and 'individuals' composing the state apparatus.

Then comes the substantial critique. Starting from that perspective, Miliband has forgotten that 'the fundamental contradiction of the capitalist system, according to Marx, is not at all a contradiction between its social character and its "private purpose", but a contradiction between the socialization of productive forces and their private appropriation'. Thus Miliband's whole analysis of the system, in its objective relations, allegedly dissolves along parameters that are typical of the sociological ideology of 'social action' rather than of Marxist analysis.

These polemical comments are justified by Poulantzas's careful consideration of Miliband's work. In reality, in Miliband's hands,

the problem of the relationship between the ideal collective capitalist and the contemporary state changes, slowly but surely, into an
empirical problem: the relationships between the state, its elites, and
the economically dominant class.[29] This looks more like C. Wright
Mills than Marx! But there is more. In reality, the recuperation of
the bourgeois theory of social action is possible in Miliband because,
while he insists on the socialization of the forces of production (the
'new' that constitutes the contemporary state), he does not seem
to grasp the fundamental fact that this socialization of the forces
of production replicates and multiplies the antagonistic dialectic
between the forces of production and the capitalist structure of
production. Indeed, for Miliband, socialization is the mediation of
the contradictions between the forces, and only the 'possible' character, juridically 'private', of appropriation reintroduces elements
of antagonism in the face of socialization. Alessandro Serafini puts
it like this:

> The civil society that he [Miliband] refers to not only consists of the
> Marxian 'set of material relations of production' but also includes ideo-
> logical and institutional relations. In short, Miliband's reference is not
> Marxian, but Gramscian. The consequences are significant and apply
> precisely to the conception of the state, its function and its situa-
> tion with respect to civil society. Between the material relations and
> the state, a third moment is inserted, a further level of mediation,
> what Miliband generically calls the 'political' level. In this context,
> the 'conditions of possibility' of the state itself are formulated; in this
> autonomous context, the bases for that consensus that makes possible
> the legitimation and the exercise of the monopoly of force by the state
> are created. This 'political' level thus becomes the positive and active
> term, the site where capitalist power finds not only justification but
> also foundation. Consequently the state is the product of this compre-
> hensive mechanism and the institutional result of this mechanism of
> struggle between ideologies and between representations of interests.
> Unlike in Marx, then, the foundation of the institutions – in the broad-
> est sense of the term – is this political level that is automatized and
> made active. Unlike in Lenin, the state is confined only to a part of the
> overall political mechanism of capital's dominion.[30]

We have seen how Poulantzas has partially grasped the substantive
limits of Miliband's approach. The arguments around methodology and the criticism of substance that I cited combine in a call for
a much more 'objective' grounding of the problem of the capitalist state. But up to what point does this happen? Up to what point
does the radical charge of 'elitism' and of 'private juridical' illusions

brought against Miliband offer the possibility of identifying the real platforms [*paliers*] for a communist theory of the state?

Some commentators criticize the cumbersome nature of Poulantzas's approach.[31] Perhaps it would have been preferable to try to identify the basis and the reason for this jumble of elements – the fact that in Poulantzas the communist theory of the state tends to be configured as a 'regional study', in a specific region, albeit one with economic predominance.[32] But in the end the regional specificity becomes so large that it seems almost like a new version of the theories of the forms of the state, while the economic predominance is objectively projected into a 'last resort' so distant as to appear insignificant. Not a word about labour processes!

But let us take a closer look. One is not interested in indicating only the illusory nature of some Althusserian methodology used by Poulantzas.[33] That its defects are such as to bring about a series of 'ideological autogeneses' for each of the 'regions' considered, so that, for each of them, the 'fundamental concept of class as a determinate relationship that is expressed in a concrete totality' is methodologically suppressed;[34] that the concern to establish a 'formal' distinction between the various aspects of the interpretation of a phenomenon ends up determining 'distinct fields of human practice and distinct theoretical spheres' where Marx sees 'levels of complexity of reality that are articulated in complex totalities of thought';[35] and that, in the end, the 'autonomy' of the state as a regional field does not find credible elements of relativity (whence 'Bonapartism' as an 'eternal' element of the bourgeois state) – well, all this can be secondary. But what is not secondary is the fact that the methodological unilaterality of Poulantzas's discourse is articulated with a substantive, clearly determined approach: still the 'autonomy of the political', not as a dialectical nexus between forces of production and capitalist structures of production but as a 'third level' between the one and the other. This means that, again, Poulantzas's methodology is functional for a specific distortion of the Marxist conception of the state, one that establishes a level of foundation of the state that is not Marx's world of production relations but the fetish of a recomposed 'civil society' – an indeterminate image of real class relations in the form of representations. The historicist and idealist cocktail of the Gramscian theory of civil society[36] unexpectedly reappears to lay the basis for a theory that resolutely claims to be anti-historicist and anti-idealistic. The Gramscian theme of 'hegemony' – the key to a sociological interpretation of the functioning of the structures of bourgeois power[37] – gets hypostatized and fixed on an 'objective' terrain, but the dialectic of that terrain presents itself in the form of ideas and mere representations of interests.[38] (Incidentally, this does a very bad service to the Gramscian conception of 'hegemony' as a hypothesis of the proletarian party's activity and victory!) Finally, the theoretical objective itself of the analysis – to fix the relative autonomy of the state vis-à-vis other regional terrains (in this case, the economic) – ends up being mystified, because relative autonomy is assumed rather than resulting from this analysis. At the limit, this 'relative autonomy' seems to be the stamp of civil society rather than of the state, the specific sign of the *foundation* of the state rather than a term that qualifies the *exercise* of state power.

Finally, if we consider the political consequences of this (or these) neo-Gramscian formulations of the communist theory of the state, we are bound to recognize that the limit I referred to is broadly reached. Here again, as in stamocap theory, the state mystifies its autonomy in relation to the antagonistic term of working-class struggle. Working-class struggle does not and cannot direct itself against the state, but has to be mediated at the level of civil society. The fight against wage labour, and then against the state as a direct social organizer of wage labour, is opposed and replaced by a model of the struggle that takes place in the world of goods distribution. The working-class foundation of Marx's analysis is neglected, and consequently the analysis of the new form of the capitalist organization of wage labour becomes increasingly unproductive and insignificant. Again, distribution is foregrounded; again, we see the whole world of representations and uncritical immediacy; again, there is political economy and politics *tout court* instead of critique of political economy. In this sense, the neo-Gramscian theories of the state lead to the repetition of stamocap theory without possessing its dark dignity, the grandeur of proletarian sectarianism.

4   Restating the problem: From distribution to production

Let us return to the themes raised at the end of section 2. So this is not simply about understanding that 'capitalist development changes the nature of the state in an essential way, and, since it continually expands the sphere of its intervention, the state acquires new functions and makes always more necessary, above all in economic life, its insertion and control'.[39] It is rather about understanding how this occurs and about relating the individual aspects of the transformation to the totality of the process of class struggle.

Now, in the 1960s, the young and (politically) heterodox Marxist critique began to address this question rather usefully. First of all, an insistent reference to Marx's methodology of the specific abstraction of the tendency and of the concrete totality[40] enabled us to redefine a correct horizon for the Marxist definition of the state – a horizon that excludes revisionist reversions and supporting arguments extraneous to the structural perspective of the analysis. Therefore, whatever the subsequent developments of the investigation, the analysis of the capitalist state has to be grounded at the level of commodity production, as an essential moment of capitalist antagonism:

> revisionist theories, political science, and many economic theories share the assumption that under capitalism the state can comprehensively and consciously regulate economic, social, and political processes. This is why the state's own sphere – in which it must appear as a 'social state', independent of capitalist production – is 'the distribution of the social product'. Here the state should be able to use its leverage to improve capitalist society, or even to move it gradually towards socialism. This kind of conception assumes that 'the sphere of distribution is independent and autonomous from the sphere of production'. Consequently production and the laws that control it should not set on distribution any limitations that fundamentally cannot be manipulated.[41]

But this claim – together with the illusions and mystifications that derive from it – is completely erroneous. In effect 'the specific element of the capitalist mode of production consists in the fact that the basis of the economic reproduction of society is the circulation of capital, and that the sphere of the distribution of incomes represents only a moment of the circulation of capital'. The 'dual character' of the process of production – as a sign of the class antagonism that presides over the capitalist organization of the direct labour process – thus infuses the entire ambit of the circulation of capital, and it is impossible to define phases or moments that render themselves, within the field of the global process, independent of or autonomous from the initial antagonism. 'Relative autonomy' of the state, they say; the state as the 'stock exchange' of the pluralistic actions (of the relations of force) that are established at the level of distribution. All this is mystification pure and simple, and can be given no credence when one considers the political life of states in advanced capitalism. Thus any attempt at a redefinition of the state has to step down from encompassing circulation of capital (and its socialization) as the scope of enlarged reproduction of antagonisms in production to encompassing direct production. This is the Marxian way: Marx's analysis of the organization of the working day and of factory legislation indicates the method and the terrain of this line of argument.[42] Thus, as in Marx's analysis, the state becomes the peak of a comprehensive dialectic between organizational and repressive aspects of the presence of the working class within capital. The concept of state emerges only dialectically from the antagonistic clash between these functions, in a situation where the mechanism of continuous tendential ideal unification of control, and also the process of profound radical alienation of the emergence of the class, increasingly co-opt the reality of the state to be the overall organizer of exploitation. At any rate, 'the questions raised above all reduce themselves in the last instance to the role played by general–historical relations in production, and their relation to the movement of history generally. The question evidently belongs within the treatment and investigation of production itself.'[43]

It should be added immediately that this reframing of the problem and this redefinition of its proper terrain do not at all exhaust the subject and, what is more, only touch on specifying the problem – namely how the state integrates into society as part of capitalist development. We know that it integrates itself antagonistically, in the sphere of circulation; we know that the socialization of production and the extension of state command over the socialization of production are moments of enlarged reproduction of the essential antagonism. But the question that now needs to be resolved is to confront the series of nexuses that open within the relations of production, to describe them in their contemporary figure, and to give them a logic of class and struggle.

During the 1960s, in the heated climate of the reconstruction of a working-class political perspective and after the definitive recognition of the crisis of Stalinism, some steps in this direction began to be taken. The German resetting of the problem – from distribution to production (the article by Müller and Neusüss was one of the most widely read texts in the German movement) – was joined by a series of Italian writings (involving Panzieri[44] and Tronti, and also *Quaderni rossi*[45] and various experiences closer to the movement[46]), which attempted to widen the project with a view to readdressing the theme of the state, reformulating the lines of research that needed to be pursued in this regard, and so on. In Italy more than in the German experience, the problem was raised not only in relation to reclaiming the thematics of circulation and production against that of distribution, or the thematics of the 'factory worker' [*operaio*] against that of the 'worker' [*lavoratore*] and of the 'citizen' – but, beyond the level of a mere theoretical hypothesis, especially as a political verification of the mechanism by which the world of distribution (together with the forces that regulate it and the reformism that optimizes its regulation) reacts to insubordinate movements in the sphere of production. From this point of view, the relative autonomy of the state re-emerged – as a category and as a function – insofar as the social development of struggles, the diffusion of insubordinate behaviours in conjunction with the expansion of the dimensions of productive work, and the deepening of its abstract character[47] exposed the real dialectic of the state in the face of struggles. Rather than being able to define itself as 'autonomous', as an internal regulator of the relation with capital, the figure of the state revealed that its function was to replace the automatic relation with capital in regulating the contradictory relationships, increasingly antagonistic nowadays, which stretch between the positions of strength of the two classes in struggle.

This means that, from the point of view of workers' struggles (that is, of the privilege bestowed in Marxism on the analysis of the antagonisms in production), a twofold process takes place concomitantly: on the one hand, the state is forced to intervene more and more heavily in production, to configure itself as a representative of social capital, to turn into a reality its tendency to embody Engels's 'ideal collective capitalist'; on the other, it increasingly regains a relative autonomy of behaviour, insofar as this unfolds on the rhythm of class struggle. But it does so, one should note, not towards the class of capitalists, not towards the exploitational logic of capitalist development, but in the face of the arguments of value and progress that contradictorily legitimated capitalist development itself. The state becomes a collective representative of capital, a substitute for the automatic relationship of social capital, a full-blown party of the bourgeoisie, when workers' struggles force it to do so by affecting the capital relation, by putting it in crisis, by devaluing its contents. But then the new relative autonomy of the state is a desire for the permanence and continuity of the power of exploitation, an exaltation of capitalist command, even in a situation of devaluation. The relative independence of the state is not a detachment from the world of capitalists but a more powerful ability to determine the crisis and destruction of value, a more powerful desire to control, with a purely repressive function, the dynamics and the consequences of a relationship of crisis.[48]

Therefore reopening the problem of the state in terms appropriate to the experience of the workers' struggle and of the present capitalist crisis means reopening it forcefully, in the terms of critique of political economy, with its grounding of analysis in the world of production, bearing in mind Engels's warning that 'the more it [the modern state] proceeds to the takeover of the productive forces, the more it actually becomes the national capitalist, and the greater the number of citizens it exploits': and thus 'the capitalist relation is not abolished but rather pushed to its extreme'. We should also bear in mind that this level of maximal rupture between the forces of production and the relations of production multiplies the destructive capacity of capital. It is this melding of the socialization of exploitation and the massification of the power to determine crisis, negative value and destruction that gives us the figure of the state in its current 'relative autonomy'.

5 Developments in the structural analysis of the state: The organizational mechanisms

In the structural definition of the state, a significant advance, whatever you think of it, was made by writers connected to the so-called Frankfurt School. Already in 1962, moving in a fairly traditional analytical framework and assimilating some famous achievements of legal sociology, Jürgen Habermas[49] pointed to the disintegration of the private principle of the market and consequent disintegration of the conception of the legal norm as an entity endowed with abstractness and generality. Where the dialectic of the public sphere was overturned by a prior and higher unity of command, where the planning of social integration and the repression of autonomies became structural to the development of modern societies, the guarantees of the state of right became pure mystification, designed to cover a plebiscitarian formation of consensus. What alternative was there to the disintegration of the civilizing and liberal function of bourgeois public opinion? None that was not purely subjective and utopian, in a situation in which every function of autonomy increasingly tended to fall under the principle of exclusion. 'Critical publicness' was now only a 'principle of hope'.

The Marxist deepening and radicalization of this Habermasian approach was not long in coming, and occurred in the fiery debates of 1968.[50] But my interest is in following, not so much the process by which the totalitarian image of the system of power emerged, as the concomitant process by which it articulates itself in the structural analysis of state functions and the way in which its ability to become a representative of the overall process of social extension of surplus value is based on a rigid mechanism of inclusion–exclusion. Valorization is not guaranteed by guaranteeing 'the political privilege of a minority that dominates both economically and by excluding and repressing articulations of need that could prejudice the system'.[51] Qua exploitation processes, valorization processes spread, then, throughout the entire state machine; capitalist valorization, reproduction of capital, circulation, realization – all tend to become one inside the category of political domination.

> We must therefore abandon that perspective that – in accordance with the tradition of the sociology of power, both in its orthodox Marxist [?] and in its Weberian forms – analysed the organization of social power according to the 'intentional' schema of the 'interested use of the means of power'. In its place, in the conditions of the regulated capitalism of the welfare state, it seems more adequate to give a 'functional' explanation of privileges and of directions of action, which meet in the 'process of valorization' of politically organized power. This change of perspective implies that the structurally privileged 'interest' of 'a ruling class' (or of its administrative adviser) should no longer be proposed as the point of reference in the analysis of systems of politico-administrative action; rather its place should be taken by a schema of 'three fundamental problems of the system', a schema whose solution for the political system is hypostatized in an 'imperative' that is objectively obligating and specific with respect to interests.[52]

The three nodes of fundamental problems are 'the node of economic stability, which includes the problems of guaranteeing full employment and balanced economic development'; 'the node of foreign politics, foreign trade and politico-military relations'; and 'the node of the loyalty of the masses, which refers to matters of internal integration of the population'.

Now, it must be clear that the fabric of the political analysis of the state is created by the interweaving of Marxian definitions about the reproduction of capital. However, the scope of this analysis, which gathers many contributions of American sociology on exclusion and marginalization[53] and is sometimes tinged with German-style catastrophism, is rigidly implanted in the analysis of production relations. The fact that certain conclusions lead to the creation, in society, of a wide context of disadvantaged interests that makes it difficult to reduce these directly to class relations does not exclude the class nature of the situation: it simply defines the trends* of capitalist socialization in a particular way, extending it in terms of class definition. If anything, the insistence on the diffusion of antagonisms accentuates the possibility of their characterization in terms of class.[54]

But thus far we are still within the problematics of the general definition of the relationship between state and civil society. The totalitarian character of this relationship, the quality of the relations, and the dynamics of the imperatives must now be articulated and analysed in their concrete interrelations. In this regard, too, the most recent literature offers us notable contributions. Claus Offe, in particular, proposes to tackle this problem of a specific articulation using a framework of two fundamental schemas: the analysis of the mechanisms of domination [*dominio*] in the system of formation of political will, and the analysis of the functions of domination in the state apparatus.

It is on the first of these schemas that, in my opinion, the analysis has made the most significant advances. J. Agnoli[55] has described, perhaps most compendiously, the process by which the mechanisms of political representation and constitutional responsibility move in alternation, having a purely mystifying function, or cancel each other out inside a tendency that increasingly makes the state into a direct instrument of capitalist valorization. This is not about denying, even in this case, the 'relative autonomy' of the state; it is simply about defining its position with respect to the function of domination. And then we shall see the whole state machine 'filtering' and 'preparing', in a rhythm of subsequent integration and necessary exclusion, the system of needs that civil society presents. The antagonisms and polarities that the process of capitalist socialization extends from the sphere of production to that of distribution must be – and are – dissolved into a pluralism that functions in favour of the mediatory recomposition of general capital. General capital – that is, the global (political) mediation of capital – articulates the rules of political participation, not giving space to alternatives that emerge from social interests but continually playing on their manipulation, opposing to them the objective and necessary rules of technical–economic development.[56]

From political representation to the organs of representation, the crisis of the parliamentary system turns over to other bodies (such as political parties and trade unions) the function of mediation, both

---

* In English in the original.

integrative and repressive, of social interests and the elimination of their potential antagonism. The state of mature capital extends its rigidly selective function through a flexible instrumentalization, which asks for – but often, indeed increasingly, does not obtain – the participation of social groups. The formation of political will is thus represented as an articulation prepared by, and in any case included in, the system of domination, through a selective mechanism that runs through social pluralism to the point of determining it.[57]

And yet, despite the perfection attained by the processes of selective integration, despite the richness and the articulation of the mechanisms, the statal operation of global capital still finds itself confronted, on a wide scale, with the emergence of unresolved and unresolvable antagonisms. Here, then, the mechanism of transmission–repression attaches itself, quite consequentially and complementarily, to the mechanism of integration–selection. Analysing the bureaucratic machine and the processes of planning, Offe focused on the component elements of the second schema – the one that concerns the state system's functions of direct domination. Here, of course, the bureaucratic–administrative apparatus is pre-eminent. Now, the advanced democracy of mature capitalist systems puts in place a system of surveys, of impulses from above, of symbolic politicization, all of which permit the effective development of administrative action even as they determine its 'political' legitimacy. The participatory selectivity imposed by the administrative machinery allows the exercise of increasingly politically legitimated repressive functions. In this context, the relative autonomy of the state once again conquers the whole of its essential density. In the 'filtering' of social interests, in the evaluation of their degree of organization, and in the subsequent decision between the alternatives of integration and repression, the state achieves the political mediation of the capitalist valorization process.[58] But all this is far from functioning only in general and formal terms: the 'state plan' substantializes, with public decision-making materiality, the individual steps of the process of valorization of capital. The flexibility of objective command seeks to make itself internal to the labour process itself; the capitalist machine becomes 'political' from the base to the top; the state becomes, in Marxian terms, a chapter of *Capital*.

But let us pause for a moment. In presenting this first aspect of the structural theory of the state (about the mechanisms of its organization), I have forced the pace somewhat, by highlighting the coherence of the approach and the effectiveness of the most innovative reading instead of giving space to features that the analysis offered by the Frankfurt School analysis insists on. A certain one-sidedness and rigidity of description, an excessive insistence on the tendential nature of the process, and, again, a kind of catastrophist anxiety – these elements are always present, they are the philosophical soul of the investigation. Yet these would be minor elements, were it not for the fact that they produce mystifying effects in the investigation itself and in its results. In fact it seems that – in the absence of an accurate analysis of the quality, extent, and dimension of productive labour in capitalist society (which is to say, in the absence of a precise definition of the degree of 'subsumption of labour') – it is precisely this tension that produces an effect of theoretical and political distortion. In almost all the authors cited, the tendency towards the political unity of the process of exploitation (in the figure of the state) generally leads to an excessive insistence on the disparity of possibilities and on the formal schema of exclusion, both of which replace the criterion of inequality that characterized direct capitalist exploitation. In this context, when the conflicts that domination must resolve can be directly traced back not to the class structure but to a horizontal schema of inequality of life environments, the very concept of domination, instead of being refound as a function, risks turning into an unmediated natural essence; and the tools of domination risk being qualified and evaluated in purely ideological terms. A real tendency thus becomes a screen to the definition of a reality that is much more concretely and articulatedly contradictory. Pursuing instead an analysis of the articulations of social labour in its figures of productive or unproductive labour, of labour that is directly or indirectly productive, especially where the mechanisms of the reproduction of labour power are concerned, would have been a far more effective way to reach a realistic definition of the organizational structure of the planned capitalist state and an adjustment between the tendency hypothesis and the actual state of things.

As it happens, structural analyses of the organization of the planned state are moving increasingly in this direction. J. Hirsch began the trend[59] – but almost silently, as if he were simply repeating and deepening in a particular field the initial hypothesis of the Frankfurt School. In reality, the analysis of the mechanisms of adaptation of the state's administrative machine to the change in the social conditions of the capitalist realization of value transferred the emphasis of the debate onto the nexus established, more or less directly, between the capitalist economic base and the state. Here planification [*il piano*] not only revealed the political necessity of showing itself and functioning as a criterion of internal discrimination of objectives vis-à-vis the economic growth of the system, but above all appeared as an initiative aimed at continuously determining a social structure suitable for the reproduction of capitalist relations of exploitation. In late capitalism, the relationship between civil society and the state cannot be anything but a strategy aimed at balanced economic growth (where balance means capitalist distribution of incomes and investments as well as qualification of needs) and at the infrastructural reproduction of both the labour force and the conditions of production (i.e. of profit). Here capitalist socialization becomes, once again, socialization of the relation of exploitation in a specific sense. Here the whole machine of the state is seen to develop from the starting point of the need to control this socialization of the capitalist relationship of exploitation. Here the analysis of the infrastructure of the capitalist circulation of goods hinges on the definition of productive labour and requires the apparatus of the state to deal with its powerful social emergence. On the other hand, the structural specificity of the relationship between capital and the state is proven negatively, so to speak, by the new figure taken by crisis. Crisis, at this level of development, now always presents itself as political crisis; and this is not because the economic materiality of crisis no longer occurs, but precisely because this specificity is so extensive, and presupposes such social conditions, that crisis can fix its own figure only in political terms. Thus the correlation between capitalist socialization and the state finds, precisely in the exaltation of the political, a class component that is no longer surmountable.[60]

A similar approach is carried even further by Jim O'Connor, a Californian author of ample German studies.[61] In advanced capitalist societies, the state has to perform functions of both accumulation and legitimation. The former tend to affirm the socialization of the costs of reproduction of both constant social capital and variable social capital. The latter, too, can be quantified in the Marxian categories of social consumption, that is, public expenditure, intended to create a linear relationship of correspondence between social demand and capitalist supply. Now, the most interesting element is the contradictoriness that opposes instances of social accumulation to instances of legitimacy. O'Connor thus pushes to the limit of contradiction the forced compatibility established in the Frankfurt School between integrative mechanisms and repressive apparatuses. This contradictoriness appears at all the levels of the state machine, from the financial and fiscal machine to the monetary machine. But all this is only allusive. In reality the contradiction is not abstract; it begins to reappear with the emergence of organized and antagonistic social forces. Here the virtuous coincidences between the profit mechanism and the financing mechanisms of public spending become impossible; the legitimacy of accumulation no longer manages to be a given; and crisis reappears – as political crisis, as crisis of the state.

We are certainly still on the terrain, somewhat left behind, of objective analysis of the capitalist structure and of the contradictions that mark it (and in parallel with it we will still have an idea of communism as planning and rationality of production). Yet a path towards overcoming and recovering the Frankfurt structural analysis seems to take shape. This is because, despite everything, inside and against that structural Moloch, the planned state of late capitalism, a reference begins to emerge to contradictions determined not so much by the relationship between capitalists and by their struggle for the distribution of profit as by the struggle between the two classes. Class struggle is introduced here, in the structural image that the Frankfurt School has given of the state.

6   Developments in the structural analysis of the state: The state in crisis theory

This is only a beginning. On other theoretical horizons, there is a re-emergence of the structural theory of the state and of its opening up to the topic of class struggle. It is as if, after having been for too long dominated by a certain materialist primitivism (in the theory of the instrumental relationship between monopolies and the state), the theory had turned around and placed its particular negation in a dialectical position that attempted to recover the specificity of the mechanisms of state functioning; and now, at the end of this journey, elements of synthesis are proposed again, in order to overcome and recompose the complexity of the analysis from the working-class viewpoint. Of course, this dialectical development is only a case of thought process and, for me, only a guide for exposition.

What is certain is that, gradually, in relation to the violent re-emergence of the elements of the capitalist crisis in the most recent cyclical phase, the centripetal unilinearity of the structural theory of the state is itself in crisis. Not, however, in the sense of denying the qualitative leap it had represented in the development of the Marxist theory of the state, namely that the state presents itself as inhering globally in development and its internal mediation is a definitive and irreversible element. But in the sense of identifying how the state – now established as a substitute for the automatic relation of capital – suffers the crisis, in what form it is involved in it, and how it reacts.

Offe tries to work out, from his point of view, a first sketch of a theory of crisis.[62] First he specifies that the ductility of the relationship between the state and individual capitals is a fundamental condition for the long-term harmonization of development and that the transactional functions assumed by the state are capable of modifying essentially the force of the economic laws of the market. Then, after having underlined the complexity and the articulation of the subsumption of capitalist development under the state, Offe explains the reappearance of crisis as a necessary effect of the transfer of regulatory functions from the market to the state. The anarchy of the public sector is the necessary correlate of the incessant rationalization of economic development. So much for the level of reopening of contradictions. Secondly, when it comes to the quality of contradictions, it should be observed (taking up the results of O'Connor's analysis) that they are determined along the aporias of the relation between processes of accumulation and the process of legitimation or, to use Offe's words, along the asymmetry between the consequences of the valorization process and the means by which it is regulated. Taking the American and German experiences as their starting point, these authors focus on two parallel phenomena: on the one hand, the marginalization of increasingly substantial quotas of labour power out of production, as a consequence of the improvement of the mechanism of production and as an effect of the strategies implemented for conflict prevention; on the other hand, the continual deepening, within these dialectical nodes, of the functional chaos of the public apparatuses and the multiplication of parasitic characteristics (bodies) in the state of mature capitalism. All this is certainly not put forward in order to revalidate revisionist theses on the autonomy of the state and on the possibility of a rationalizing reform; on the contrary, it is put forward rather to reconfirm the impossibility for reformism to control and transform the state of mature capitalism.[63] The tendency of the planned state of capital to determine its own stability through the achievement of an adequate measure of general social surplus value, of a complete administrative and planning rationality, and of an effective and dynamic system of legitimation thus clashes with increasingly strong critical contradictions, which take place at the level of the planned structure of the state and bring about an implacable series of failures there.

With these sketches of a theory of the crisis, the structural approach to the analysis of the state undoubtedly takes a big step towards a dialectical dynamicization of the image produced. But is this enough to determine the actually class-related nature of the crisis and of the state? The question grows all the more meaningful as attempts at institutional and sociological closure of the theory of crisis can develop on this same terrain.[64] On the other hand, is it not the case that Offe's arguments represent one point, and only one point, in the transition to a systematization of the theory of crisis that is more consistent from the perspective of class struggle?

Let us examine one part of the problem. Offe expressly declares that the process of accumulation must change its class-related nature, since it is now formally a political process. In fact, if we move within the horizon of an accumulation organized by essentially administrative means and with forms of social mediation other than the mere production of goods, the parameters of the class definition have to change, just as the sequences of the determination of the crisis change.[65] Here, however, Offe's argument comes to a standstill, because the call to consciousness, to its collective recompositions and reconfigurations, is not sufficient to solve a problem of class definition. Offe's analysis comes to a halt, in a vacuum of class determination; but this has an immediate consequence for the development of the analysis. And it is the case that the political system of capitalism, too, relies on its stability or falters in a void of material determinations during crisis: what gets lost once you exclude the 'old' conception of the antagonism between the two classes is the driving rule of the system. The restatement of the problem of crisis within the general structures of state structure and the progressive unification of political and economic processes do not solve the problem of the class-related nature of the process, of its dynamism, of its direction and meaning. They simply restate it at a higher level – and this must be underlined as an extremely important moment.[66]

So what governs this dynamism, and the crisis? How can the problem be restated, once the acquisition of the planned and global nature of the contemporary state has been settled?

On the one hand, the problem has been addressed – and already answered – with special insistence on the residual relationship between the state and the dialectical whole of individual capitals.[67] Altvater in particular has tried, with great skill, to demonstrate that, if, in accordance with the Frankfurt theses, the state cannot be conceived of just as a political or institutional instrument to be used by capital, the special form of the amalgam impressed by the state on the social existence of capital must encompass the entire competitive dialectic of individual capitals. In this context, the law of value and the effectiveness of its functioning cannot be thought of as replaced and abolished, but simply modified. In what sense? In the sense that the state, while confirming and validating the functioning of the market through an infrastructural and transactional intervention, on the other hand presents itself as a kind of vacuum, as a 'non-capitalist' in a society of capital, as a 'negative limit' of value formation. It is a dialectical relationship, biunivocal: the state is simultaneously a condition (totalizing) and an effect (of the functioning of the law of value, as the law of discrepancy and the averaging of individual capitals). The autonomization of capital is therefore intrinsic to the nature of the capitalist process but is placed in a negative, dialectically negative, relationship with the tendency of capitalist development towards valorization. The state guarantees capitalist relations (and guarantees them increasingly) insofar as it acts in a non-capitalist form, and is therefore not a direct element of valorization.

The theory of crisis is thus established on the basis of these premises, and it is from them that the basic nature of crisis is drawn – with greater or lesser intensity, depending on the weight given to the dialectic of individual capitals. To give just a few examples: in W. Müller[68] the intensity of the subordination of the state plan to the project of single capitals is at a maximum; here, therefore, the crisis starts to move again as a crisis of imbalances and circulation. In Altvater, on the other hand,[69] since the dialectic between the state and the law of market value is viewed as one between coequal terms [*paritariamente*], according to biunivocal tensions, the crisis is represented qualitatively. Its proper representation is stagflation, since it brings together two reasons: state intervention up to the saturation of the material (negative, infrastructural) conditions of production; crisis of quality in the value of capitalist production, since that can be determined only by the functioning of the market. In short, the state, by intervening in Keynesian fashion, can offer salvation from collapse but, since it (the state) is not an element of valorization, it brings about stagnation or new forms of crisis – while development can derive only from the immanent forces of capital. Finally, P. Mattick,[70] while assuming that the relationship between state and private capitals is fundamental and considering private capital to be the driving force in this process, does not insist on the alternative and sees interdependence as increasing, or at any rate intensifying in the crisis phase.

I think that at this point an essential alternative has been reached in the analysis conducted here. Let us look at the passage in our old friend Engels where he sees the state shaping itself as the ideal collective capitalist, with a view to retaining private production without control over private property: the more this ideal collective capitalist 'proceeds to the takeover of the productive forces, the more it actually becomes the national capitalist, and the greater the number of citizens it exploits'.[71] It is clear that this description must be taken in dynamic and tendential terms, but it is also clear that, in the process, the transformation of the state into a productive essence is determined with precision and therefore two lines in it must be examined: the decreasing importance of the relationship of the state with individual capitals and the permanently deepening and widening extension of the process of exploitation as regulated by the state. Now, we have seen how structural theory has followed and described the expansion of the exploitation process and its representation within the state, but has failed to determine the specificity of exploitation relations in the social field, and thereby has kept the image of the planned state of exploitation below the threshold of insignificance. But what does it mean to move away from criticizing this inclusiveness and to go back to pinpointing the origins of valorization, as well as those of the crisis, in the market mechanisms? What does it mean to reduce this planned state to a merely 'conditioning' or 'residual' element in the production of surplus value? The two positions are, fundamentally, one: either one denies the planned nature of the contemporary state (but only the blind would do that) or, if one admits to it, it is not possible surreptitiously to reintroduce a central dialectic with individual capitals – and private ones, for that matter. The contradiction between the state and individual capitals will obviously be borne in mind but treated as subordinate – as the documentary material indicates. As a clear and sure alternative, the analysis must be based on the 'ideal and collective' complex of capital, on the state as its representation, discriminating within that totality, according to class lines and the expansion of the working-class point of view, the real mechanisms of exploitation as they emerge in this new dimension. The structural analysis of the state must be perfected and completed with an analysis of crises and with a definition of the technical and political composition of the proletariat – by reworking Marx's theory of value in this direction.

The same goes for crisis theory. Indeed, from this point of view, a series of elements in the definition of crisis – elements grasped in the structural school, yet often too formally and from an objectivist structural perspective, anyway – regain a material grounding and a general meaning. Within the qualitative leap that capital and the state make – according to Marx's prediction and structuralism's description – the whole structure of exploitation makes a qualitative leap. The relevance of subjective moments (in Marx's and Lenin's sense: as relevance of all class behaviours) and the emergence of the subjective point of view of class become, then, the most decisive and important elements from which analysis can develop and be completed.[72] This is so from the point of view of method, and to the definitive rejection of positions that, in their search for a dialectical path of analysis, continue to forget that Marx's dialectic covers the objective circuits of capital only insofar as it is based on the dialectic of exploitation, on the antagonistic relationship between the two classes.[73]

From the point of view of substance, the necessary modification of the class-related nature of a process of accumulation that has also become formally political – to put it in Offe's language – leads the analysis back to the definition of the new way in which productive labour (and its categories) configures itself, to the new figure of the proletariat, and so on.[74]

There is a lot of work to be done, but only in this way would it be possible to regain, with a correct image of the state, the scale and the antagonistic relations of class.

7   An aside: Quibbles, allusions and self-criticism of bourgeois theory

The most remarkable thing is that, while the communist theory of the state looks at the presence of the working class in a purely liminal manner, bourgeois theory – even though bound by its programme to deny or mystify it, or somehow to mediate it – is attracted to it, being coercively obliged to measure its own validity against its own political efficacy. And, if bourgeois theory will never be able to pay heed to working-class subjectivity – that is, in Marxian language, to the totality of working-class behaviours, be they spontaneous or conscious, specific to labour power or to the party, and somehow active in the dialectic of capital – as a theoretical fact, nevertheless the approach to the materiality of this emergence and to the sequences that derive from it is, paradoxically, more alert to the bourgeoisie than what we see in the field of working class theory. This is not the place to examine why this is so – how many and how varied are the misdeeds of revisionism. It would be more interesting to consider how bourgeois theory approaches the problematic of the state when it bears in mind that massive presence of the working class, as if it were an event to be exorcised.

It is now well known that, between Keynes and the New Deal, the development of the theory of the state was conditioned by a reflection on the causes of the great capitalist crisis, which followed the Bolshevik conquest of power and lasted through to the 1930s. The resulting conception of the state is based, not only on a huge effort of technical restructuring of class composition (the shift from the skilled worker to the mass worker), but also on the attempt to make the state a dynamic machine of planned and reformist intermediation of capitalist development.[75] Economic science bends to this innovation of the capitalist state, and so do the applied sciences of social exploitation (sociology, human engineering, urban planning, and so on). But in Keynesianism the fundamental hypotheses of development are confirmed anyway: the dualism of the fundamental perception seeks to translate and recompose itself into a continuous and stable mediation, into a restoration of the fundamental categories of capital: profit, development, expanded reproduction. And the 'stagnationist' school does not change the Keynesian approach too much either: the pessimism of predictions does not transform the theoretical framework.[76] To arrive at a modification of the theoretical framework, more time had to pass – time riddled with tragic events, from the fall of residual illusions of equilibrium to the emergence of an otherwise irrepressible working class and proletarian power. The complete dialecticalization of the image of capital is thus the result of bourgeois economic science during the period that followed the second great imperialist war. In what terms is this scientific development given? What are its effects on the capitalist image of the state?

The work of P. Sraffa, the most eminent theoretical figure among bourgeois innovators in the field of economic action, is well known.[77] He starts from a rejection and critique of any attempt by classical bourgeois economics to elaborate a market theory, since he considers the transition from the formation of profit rates in terms of included labour value to a theory of the general level of profit to be irresolvable. The optimistic Keynesian conclusion about the possibility of reconstructing the categories of capital is destroyed here through an analysis that dissolves the possibility of capitalist mediation for all the relations between defining elements of capital – all except one: 'the rate of a profit remains a linear function of the wage'.[78] Consequently economic theory becomes a conscious theory of distribution in which any endogenous element for determining the quantities of distribution is lost, while the exogenous nature of the power relations between classes decisively takes the upper hand. As Napoleoni notes, from this point of view Sraffa simply offers 'a justification of principle to all the contemporary attempts to close the economic discussion within the limits of preparing the practical instruments of planning'.[79] Others, more maliciously, will argue that Sraffa's work is simply an extension of the algebra of Leontyev, the great Menshevik planner.

Now, a point to be noted: what comes centre-stage, in the face of a dissolution of the categories of capital through confrontation with an unrestrained movement of the wage variable, is the figure of the planned state. Where the category of capital has no capacity for mediation, the category of state comes to replace it. But, again, the state is here implicitly portrayed as in the Marxist view of structural theory – that is, not as a mere substitute for the rule of the market but as a specific innovation, as an ability to determine, albeit only between the power relations that govern distribution, the elements of valorization. The concept of capital is reconstructed on the state; the concept of value is no longer either substance or measure, but simply the will to mediate social antagonisms, a will expressed by the state. By way of a paradoxical confirmation, the economist adds: 'The best way to confront the theory of distribution, introducing again the reality of the class struggle into this fundamental problem of political economy, seems to be, then, to combine Sraffa's relation between rates of wage and rates of profit with the little we know – mostly from Marx – about the interrelations between real and monetary phenomena.'[80] This is like saying, let us force further the exogeneity of the capital–class relationship, let us bring it even more on the horizon of that powerful and totalitarian mystification that is money and the state.

Thus there is a theoretical itinerary between Keynes and Sraffa that, while confirming the planned reality of the state as the only alternative to the disaggregation of the market, reveals, increasingly and with ever fewer illusions, the antagonistic nature of this totalitarian reality of the state. Working-class and proletarian subjectivity – as a total exogeneous element, yet always present in the system – is what the bourgeois science of the economic process and of its regulation by the state must increasingly absorb and reveal.

But there is more. A similar itinerary is not only carried out at the highest levels of capitalist awareness; it is also – albeit sometimes along narrow paths and between quagmires – the journey accomplished by that obliging and servile bourgeois science that is law. In this case too, the crisis after the first great imperialist war had brought about significant modifications, culminating – within the New Deal laboratory – in a definitive shift of the law vis-à-vis the state. I mean that the law had increasingly attempted to transform itself, in the area of institutions and with the support of realist theories, as a function of the organization of consensus for particular and concrete purposes of reform. It was a democratic administrativization of law, as they put it: an attempt to privilege procedures over norms, reforming objectives over normative repressiveness, consensual processes of pluralism over the authoritarianism of the centralized legal system. From this point of view, New Deal democratic interventionism is a Keynesian experiment in law; it is radically different from the traditional interventionism of both liberal and fascist regimes – a shift of the law vis-à-vis the state, as was said. And in fact it happens that the rule of law [*il stato di diritto*], that is, the state justified by the pre-existence of a legal system designed to guarantee and protect public and private rights [*diritti*], democratically reappropriates the law [*il diritto*], transforming it into one of its functions and attempting to operate the system of protections and guarantees retrospectively, dynamically, not formally but in substance. The appeal of this project must have been enormous, if it is true that a whole group of European-educated formalist jurists, who came into contact with the New Deal experience through the emigration of the 1930s, accepted it as the hypothesis of their discourse. And I'm not talking only about the likes of Neumann or Friedrich, but in the first place about Kelsen, whose final theory is all laboriously bent on the attempt to solve the problem of the execution of the valid act in a dynamic and procedural form. In this case, the circularity of normative and executive acts becomes an effective key to democratizing the system. The end of liberal guaranteeism [*garantismo*] is recorded and transfigured in the attainment of a juridical ideology of power whereby the elements of validity and legitimacy are all internal to the system – one gathers, insofar as the system covers the entire flow of social materiality that it regulates. A Kelsenian utopia? Of course – so much so that, again, as in Abbé Saint-Pierre and in Kant, the investigation concludes in cosmopolitanism, in the declared utopia of an international moralizing function of the law, foundation of all orderings and legitimation of the work of jurists.

But 'international ordering' means Bretton Woods, means imperialism, and so on![81] And also, if we turn to this juridical translation of Keynesianism into domestic systems, here too the effects are paradoxical. The kind of democratic push that allows the reversal of the traditional connection between state and law, as given in the rule of law, actually concludes with an affirmation of the totalitarian character of the state, which, while it has little to do with traditional legitimism, nevertheless renews its definitive and formal characteristics. It would seem that the reformist shift of the law in the state – a shift imposed by the capitalist need to recognize and co-opt potentially subversive subjects – in the end comes to establish a disproportionate eminence of the state over the law, of legitimation over legality, such that we find here again the contours of the figure of the state described in structural theory.[82] This completes a trajectory that, while recognizing that the end of the rule of law corresponds to the end of the function of the market and while democratically attempting to accept the subject's participation in the legal system, in reality reshapes the state, accentuating its centralizing, bureaucratic and authoritarian characteristics. Schmitt's re-evaluation goes alongside that of Kelsen: decisionism and jurisprudential realism are coupled, the technocratic attitudes and the cult of efficiency combine with declarations of democratic good faith.[83]

However, the step forward was taken. In the juridical mystification of class relations, the adversary, with a new entity and a general (antagonistic) inherence in the system of power, was recognized and mystified again, at a higher level.

Thus it seems clear in broad outline that, in two strategic areas such as political economy and legal science, bourgeois science, apart from touching on a correct definition of the new characteristics of class antagonism, proposes a context of mediation and definitions that come singularly close to the reality of the state, in order to mystify it – and at the same time is hardly perceived from the proletariat's theoretical point of view. Obviously, this is not about asking for consensus or support for bourgeois science; it is rather about arming oneself to attack and destroy it. But this is possible only when the true dimensions of the contemporary state are known. So it must be said that, except for their Marxist point of view, revisionism of the stamocap type, versions of neo-Gramscianism, and the various objectivist and economistic waves of structuralist theory are less than fit for purpose.

This is because, if nothing else, bourgeois science is always animated by a solid class hatred that allows it to identify the adversary – that formidable subjective reality, the massified proletariat of developed capitalist societies. Through this hatred, it comes closer to the real nature of things than do all too many 'Marxists'!

8   Restatements of the problem: State, class struggle and communist transition

Too often there is talk of a crisis of the planner state. The discussion is messy and risks throwing out the baby with the bathwater. This is because the crisis of planning procedures, which is as strong in Anglo-Saxon countries as in Europe,[84] has no tendency to mean that the progression towards the figure of the state as the total representative of collective capital has halted. Rather the crisis of the planner state is an incentive to take another step forward, to make a new qualitative leap in the relationship between the state and capitalist production. But in any case it is not a reopening of the competition between individual capitalists, a revaluation of market rules, or a diminution of the power of automatic intervention. The necessity of state intervention in the large aggregates of capitalist production is rather pushed to the maximum; the determination of the conditions of production and the setting of transactional functions on the movement of commodities are expanded and consolidated. When we talk about the end of the planner state without clarifying the meaning and the scale of the crisis, two secondary distortions and a fundamental one occur. One distortion is typical of legal fetishism: it consists in treating legal processes as structural phenomena, and hence in inferring, from the insufficiency and defeat of the planning procedures, a blockage of the real capitalist processes. A second distortion is committed insofar as one is aware of not seeing how the development of the planned state of collective capital still makes use of legal instruments, periodically enhancing their instrumentality and functional conditioning: the functional chaos of the state's programming machine is anyway marked by its class logic. But these are secondary distortions. The fundamental issue is the accreditation of a false image of capitalist development. The tired old image of the individual capitalist is opposed to the working-class objective of the destruction of the state as quintessential representative of capitalist power; the faded banner of 'socialism' is unfurled, and the despised weapons of opportunism come to the fore.

So what does the crisis of the planner state mean? In what sense, and why, is there a crisis in the procedural tools of programming as a comprehensive whole, as a set with constitutional relevance (and indeed, taken individually, they are often able to operate)?

In general, the crisis of the planner state means crisis of the Keynesian state as a project of state intervention for capitalist development – a project based on a policy of large-scale regulation of income, on an essentially financial instrumentation, and on an ideology tinged with socialism This crisis is mainly brought about by the insufficient presence of the state in the economic mechanism and by the insufficient automatism of intervention in the face of a level of working-class and proletarian struggles that exploit the terrain of planning, both in terms of simple and direct political rupture (quality of the demands) and in terms of breaking the capitalist proportions of the processes of reproduction (quantity of the demands). In other words, in many of the new situations of planned capital, the inherence of the instruments of participation and selection has not been effecient enough; the capitalist apparatus for containing and overturning the attack from the working class has not been able to get mobilized through an appropriate dosage of repressive tools and technological innovation, of political consensus and continuous prevention of conflict. In this situation, the working-class struggle, taking advantage of the massive support provided by the struggles of the international proletariat, has been able to undermine programming and to initiate processes conducive to a radical crisis of the system. The fall in the rate of profit that is a typical consequence of the development of the capitalist mode of production, has thus been joined by a mass attack on profit that, apart from directly affecting the mechanisms of valorization, has brought about the end – or at least the weakening – of all the old routes taken to restore the rate and mass of profit. For the first time in its history, capital has had to endure an attack of such proportions that the economic laws of development and crisis have been defeated. The classic patterns of the economic science of capital – inflation, recession, unemployment, crisis, restructuring, development – can work now only if strengthened by a surplus of power. Their spontaneity is reversed; what is now spontaneous from the point of view of science and capitalist experience is the contemporaneity of contradictory sequences. What is now spontaneous is, paradoxically, the multiplication and extended reproduction of the crisis through structures of integration, in relation to the interlaced compactness of the functions and structure of the mature capitalist state: an input of workers' struggles is matched by a process of conversion that is multiplicative, reproduces the individual motivating factors for the crisis, brings about institutional chaos and, finally, represents a comprehensively critical output, itself a producer of new changes in social struggles and in any case a suitable condition for the communication and circulation of struggles.

In this type of crisis and in these power relations between the classes, the route for capital is to intensify even further the link between the state and global capital. The manoeuvre of restructuring can be carried out only insofar as the state, going beyond its Keynesian balances with global capital, stresses its presence within the production machine itself – that is, accepts the need to 'reinforce' the valorization processes with the entire range of instruments at its disposal. A political 'valorization' renders the valorization of capital real. Within this trend, both the capitalist as overseer of a production sector and the toolkit for his command over the production process (technicians, foremen, line supervisors, etc.) become 'public officials': an emanation of state power, a reinforcement of the rules of productive command. The same applies to the instruments of consensus (political and trade union figures of consensus). In the meantime, new programming techniques are being formed on the basis of this new fabric of power. This means programming not for large aggregates in terms of a socialist reinstatement of consensus but programming along internal lines, through a focused quest for consensus that separates, purely politically, sections of workers from other sections, then selects and controls them inasmuch as it organizes and reorganizes social production, and so on.

Perhaps one catches these phenomena in their utmost radicality and tendential expression in West Germany, on the basis of a specific political history and a series of integration processes that have no equal in any other developed capitalist country. Perhaps this derives basically from the fact that Keynesianism (which had an interesting kinship with Nazism as well) was not a fundamental policy in postwar Germany, since a constitutional structure of the social state of labour had been imposed since the period of Allied occupation.[85]

But let me return to the problem, or rather its restatement – namely to the fact that the fundamental acquisitions of the structural theory of the state are confirmed by the phenomenology of crisis and by the analysis of the processes of restructuring (on the capitalist side). But the theoretical–political key to solving the problem is simply hinted at here. It is necessary to deepen it, theoretically and politically. It will not be possible to do it in the present article. But it may be useful to indicate the areas in which, in my opinion, the research should go deeper.

First of all, the political terrain: here it seems possible to perceive a radical change in the way in which the materialist analysis of the full range of class relations must proceed. All the phenomena that I have mentioned, from the point of view of political economy as well as from that of the theory of the state, seem to push the critique towards the determination of a subject of development and crisis that can no longer be defined just as a complex of the dialectical rules of the realization of capital. That set of rules has dissolved, it seems, and the series of phenomena regulated by development and by the capitalist crisis seems to reveal a radicalness of the antagonism present in the process that can no longer be reduced dialectically. This substantial modification of the political process is signalled by capital and is taken as foundational by reformism.[86] This radical modification of the fabric of the capital relation – whereby we witness, in all advanced capitalist countries, a substantial dualism of powers, new and permanent, as a political overdetermination of the era – is experienced primarily on the terrain of working-class autonomy: all the objectives and all the behaviours of working-class autonomy are determined by it. But this fact reopens precisely the political problem – which consists in the solution to an alternative: on the capitalist and reformist side, we are offered the foundation and exercise of a state power capable of integrating the working class as a function of the resumption of development, in a form radically antagonistic to the emergence of working-class power. One has to emphasize this: today development passes only through the destruction of the autonomy of the working class; Nazism is a necessary component of power. The other pole of the alternative is clear: there is no workers' struggle that is not immediately a struggle on the terrain of transition, a struggle for communism, a struggle for the abolition of the state. Centring the discussion on transition,[87] deepening the analysis of the present reality of the dualism of power, relating every discussion of organization to the question of power – this becomes the primary political task.

In the present political and economic crisis, this type of alternative imposes itself with absolute urgency and intensity. The state figure to which we are heading is such as to offer us development only as a complete destruction of workers' autonomy. The reformist price of the operation – in the countries where it has to be paid – is not excessive: this kind of problem gets solved at the sociological and electoral levels of change of political class! But the state that defines itself in this crisis is instead, if you will, an even more structurally coherent figure than the German comrades have managed to define in the face of their terrible experience. It is laughable when you hear talk of fascistization of the state from those who are already working to stick the label 'criminal' onto the struggles of the working class! We should rather understand that this process of restructuring the state as a force capable of breaking the class autonomy, of eliminating it through an internal division couched in reformist terms or through technological marginalization – well, that this process is advancing vigorously.

To think that there are still people who imagine capital as essentially unplanned! They have very little imagination, and especially a stunted, rose-tinted image of capitalist processes, which are processes of exploitation, destruction and domination before being anything else and as a condition of development. Or do they imagine the transition from capitalism to communism as an easy path? But how is that transition, then? In any event, capitalist planning is there and is solid; it also lives on the functional chaos of the state's ordering. For, at these levels of industrial integration, there is no capital that is not planned – and not for development, but for domination; it is planned for development only when the working class begins to be so strong that there is no domination [*dominio*] without development. But here struggle appears again: struggle for the destruction of the working class and the restructuring of the state with this purpose, struggle for planning the destruction of autonomy, for planning a recovery of the rate and mass of profit.

On this terrain, which is directly political, research will have to go deeper and the problem will have to be reformulated. But the same holds also for another terrain, closely linked to this one. This is the terrain of in-depth study of the critique of political economy. Marx left us with an image of the state in which, to use Engels's words, the public management of private property reproduces capital and deepens exploitation. Today we are moving increasingly on this terrain. But what opens up on it is the level of class struggle, which neither Marx nor Engels could have foreseen. The relations that open up at this point between persistence in a situation of duality of powers, emergence of a working-class power antagonistic to capitalist power, and the theory of exploitation (the theory of value) must be studied more in depth. The state as a collective capitalist is the manager of exploitation; it is the planner of all exploitation, according to a function of the law of value that anticipates a socialist transformation, a management in terms of average profit (tendentially equal to surplus value). But if this is what the state is, if the state is forced into this by workers' struggles, a situation never recorded before in the history of capital, if, in the presence of these struggles, equalization and the averaging of value decrease, in that case again we shall have to reprise the entire analysis and repropose it on the terrain of the critique of political economy. In other words, we shall have to require from critique a rereading of value theory at levels at which its zeroing begins to present itself as a real horizon, where the attack of the working class on the operation of the law of value is massive. And what is the state at this point, as a collective capitalist?

To develop this discussion, it may be worth taking up here and reversing the point of view that we found in Altvater.[88] Now, there is in Altvater – albeit from a strictly objectivist point of view – a strong insistence on the 'liminal', 'residual' character of state intervention in the capitalist economy. He does not deny the planning intervention of the state, but qualifies it in extra-economic terms. The limitation of his position seems to be that, after the state itself is seen as a planning power, this extra-economic reduction of the state does not grasp the political and dualistic nature of the capital relationship. But now let us try a fresh approach to Altvater's intuition, from a dialectical point of view. We find that the parasitic and terroristic residue of the state of capitalists will reappear as a direct function of the critical difficulties of capital in producing surplus value, as a direct function of the level of workers' struggles and their intensity, as a direct function of the new form in which the fall and the flattening of the rate of profit occur today. Political analysis can follow this process by focusing on the 'dual nature' presented by capitalist production summarized in the figure of the mature capitalist state. 'Dual nature' means not only the reappearance of class antagonism at every level of the capitalist synthesis but also – today, in crisis, and especially in the light of its permanent working-class matrix – an exacerbation of the antagonism and divergence of the terms of the synthesis.

Thus the highest figure that capital has managed to produce for its state is also the outer limit of the significance of the capitalist organization of social labour. At the moment when the rationality of planned domination is attributed to the state of capital, the general purposes of this domination are reduced to control and destruction. And all this – if you like – because of the irrepressible emergence of an antagonistic power.

It is worth continuing to analyse these matters, and above all taking action.

3

Labour Value*

Crisis and Problems of Reconstruction in Postmodernity

1. In the Marxist tradition, the theory of value occurs in two forms. The first is the theory of abstract labour present in all commodities, labour being, then, the common substance of all activities of production. From this perspective, all labour is reduced to abstract labour, which makes it possible to represent with clarity, behind all the particular forms that labour might take at given times, a global social labour power capable of being transferred from one use to another according to social needs and whose importance and development depend ultimately on society's capacity for producing wealth. Marxism moves from this qualitative vision to a quantitative conception, centred on the problem of measuring the value of labour. 'Magnitude of value expresses . . . the connection that exists between a certain article and the portion of the total labor time of society required to produce it',[1] and this can be expressed in units of 'simple labour'. The main task of value theory arises out of this definition of value as quantity. The problem it raises is that of identifying the laws that regulate the distribution of labour power between the various sectors of production in a society of producers of commodities. To use a modern expression, the law of value is therefore essentially a theory of general equilibrium, first developed with reference to the production of simple goods and subsequently adapted to capitalism.[2] One of the main functions of the law of value is to make it clear that, in a commodity-producing society, although there may be neither

* Originally published as 'Valeur-travail: Crise et problèmes de reconstruction dans le postmoderne', *Futur Antérieur* 10 (1992): 30–6; visit https://www.multi tudes.net/Valeur-travail-crise-et-problemes.

centralization nor coordination in the way choices are made, there is an order – not chaos, pure and simple. The job of the law of value is to explain how all this happens and what results from it. The law of value therefore gives rationality to the operations that the capitalists carry out on the market blindly, through the play of competition, the pressures they exert on one another, and the ravages and devastations that ensue. The law of value is the preservation of social equilibrium amid the tumult of its accidental fluctuations.[3] It follows that, where the distribution of productive activity is subject to conscious control, the law of value loses some of its importance. The law of planning can take its place. 'In the economics of a socialist society the theory of planning should hold the same basic position as the theory of value in the economics of a capitalist society. Value and planning are as much opposed, and for the same reasons, as capitalism and socialism'.[4] Walras thought so too.

2.   However, in Marx the law of value comes in a second form too, as the law of the value of labour power. What does this second form of the law of value involve? It involves considering the value of labour not as a figure of equilibrium but as a figure of antagonism, the subject of a dynamic rupture of the system. In Marx's entire work, both before and after what is known as his theoretical 'caesura', the concept of labour power is considered a valorizing element of production, in a manner that is relatively independent of the functioning of the law of value. This means that the unit of value is first identified in the relation to 'necessary labour', which is not a fixed quantity but a dynamic element of the system. Qualified historically, necessary labour is determined by the struggles of the working class; it is therefore the product of the struggle against wage labour, of the effort to transform labour, to lift it out of its poverty. Thus a second point of view is formed, which makes the law of value not a law of equilibrium of the capitalist system but, on the contrary, the engine of its constitutional disequilibrium. From this perspective, we have to think of the law of value as a part of the law of surplus value, as an element that triggers the constitutional crisis of equilibrium. When the law of value applies to the whole of capital development, it generates crisis – not only a crisis of circulation and disproportion (as such, these crises can be related to the model of system equilibrium), but a crisis provoked by struggles, by the subjective disequilibrium of the cycle, by the impossibility of containing the growth of demand – in other words by the needs and desires of the subjects. In this framework, the law of value and surplus value can be seen as a dialectical

law of struggles, of continuous destructuring and no less continuous restructuring of the cycle of capitalistic development – and at the same time as the law of composition and reorganization of the working class as a power [*puissance*] of transformation.

3.   These two forms of the law of value are presented and articulated differently in Marx's work. The first form was developed especially by the different, but no less homogeneous schools that came one after another between the Second and the Third International; and it was definitively consecrated in the Soviet concept of planning. The second form of the law of value and surplus value developed in heterodox revolutionary Marxism and was especially studied, deepened and applied in Italian *operaismo* [workerism] during the decade 1960–70. Even in its second form, the law of value has always retained its dialectical structure. The thesis I would like to formulate here is that, in the development of class composition, throughout the maturation of capitalism until the postindustrial period, the first form of the law of value is exhausted and joins the second form of the law. But, fundamentally, at the very heart of this junction the law of value is radically renewed, going definitively beyond the structure and the dialectical reality of the definition.

4.   The extinction of the first form of value comes about through the deepening of its internal contradictions. The first contradiction is the one that opposes 'simple labour' to 'qualified or complex labour'. The latter cannot be reduced to a multiplier of the former, taken as unit of measurement. Thus arises the paradox in which the highest use value of skilled labour, that is, its highest productivity, seems to be deduced from, rather than to explain, the value of its product. The second contradiction sets up an opposition between 'productive labour' and 'unproductive labour'. Productive labour is that which produces capital, unlike unproductive labour. But this definition is completely reductive when it comes to the concept of productivity, of productive force in general. Indeed, productive labour in general is defined by being inscribed in cooperation more than by its relation to the formal quantities of the simple labour units that it brings together; and this is all the more so as labour has been subsumed under capital. It is cooperation that makes labour productive; and cooperation increases as the forces of production develop. Finally, the third contradiction lies in the fact that the productive labour of intellectual and scientific labour power cannot be reduced either to the simple sum of simple labour or to cooperation, complex as that may be. Intellectual

and scientific labour expresses creativity. Henceforth, these contradictions are real, in other words not only do they represent logical contradictions of the system, they also follow the evolution of capitalist development where the contradictions become concrete aporias. Thus, while the distinction between simple labour and complex labour applies in the phase of simple cooperation, it becomes aporetic in the phase of manufacture; the distinction between productive and unproductive labour applies to manufacturing and becomes aporetic in large-scale industry; as for the productive value of intellectual and scientific labour, in the postindustrial period it becomes hegemonic to the exclusion of any other productive figure. It is obvious that, as this evolution progresses, it becomes impossible to consider the law of value as a measure of the general productivity of the economic system and as a standard of its equilibrium.

5.   We can consider the extinction of the law of value differently, from the angle of a convergence of the first two forms of the law. In the second form of the law, the use value of labour power was considered to be the determining factor in the dynamics of capitalist development. This means that, through the relative independence of its variations, general labour power constrains capital to a permanent reorganization of exploitation, to an ongoing intensification of productivity, and to an increasingly global extension of its dominion. The first process – intensive integration – is characterized by the evolution of capitalism towards ever higher levels of organic composition of the productive structure – from the extraction of absolute surplus value to the extraction of relative surplus value, from industrial capital to financial capital, and so on. The second process – the global extension of domination – is characterized by the evolution of capitalism as it passes from the formal subsumption of labour to the real subsumption of society within capital. The second form of the law of value therefore gives rise to a kind of natural history of capital, governed by the dialectic between the use value of labour power and the process of capitalist subsumption. This is a bad dialectic, which posits a relative independence of labour at the heart of capitalist development, up to the maximum integration (intensive and extensive) of the use value by capital. It is therefore a bad dialectic that makes the evolution of the use value of labour power the keystone of the universal extension of exchange value. But, once the whole exogenous dimension of the use value of labour power has been reduced to exchange value, how can the law of value still exist and have any validity?

6.   We can also look at the convergence and the extinction of two forms of the law of value from another angle. The concept of value was originally thought of as temporal measurement of productivity. But under what form can time become a measure of the productivity of social labour? If social labour covers the whole of life and involves all sectors of society, how can time measure the totality in which it is involved? We are really dealing with a tautology. After having demonstrated its inability to measure qualitative difference (cooperative, intellectual, scientific) in the labour process, the law of value demonstrates its inability to distinguish between the whole of life (or relations of production and reproduction) and the entirety of time from which it is woven. When the time of life has entirely become production time, who measures what? The development of the law of value in its second form leads to the real subsumption of productive society under capital: when exploitation reaches such dimensions, its measurement becomes impossible. Hence the extinction follows of both the first and the second figures of the law of value.

7.   The fact that the law of value can no longer measure exploitation does not mean that exploitation has disappeared. What has disappeared is only the dialectical form of the law of value, that is, the form of the equivalence of simple quantitative elements, of the measurement of the process, of the constitution of development. The law of value remains as the law of surplus value, and therefore as a legal norm and as a political law, as command and control of society in capitalist subsumption. Exploitation therefore finds itself beyond any economic measurement. Its economic reality is fixed in terms that are purely political; exploitation is a function of a process of social reproduction that has for its purpose the maintenance and the reproduction of capitalist command. The concept of measurement withers and dies: the reproduction of the capitalist system is organized according to processes of disciplinarization and control of society and its various parties. Thus the material constitution of labour power and of the working day, in the society of real subsumption, can be understood and managed only from the starting point of the organization of force, from the point of view of politics, of political constitution. Capital exercises its power over the society of real subsumption only in political forms (monetary, financial, bureaucratic, administrative). It is by exercising command over communication that capital exercises command over production – which means that there is no longer a theory of production that is distinct from the pragmatics of the government of production, and there is no longer a

theory of the social organization of labour, of the working day, of the distribution of income that is distinct from command over the whole.

8. The law of value as a dialectical law (as a law of measurement) has therefore definitively imploded; but exploitation remains. It is an exploitation all the more ferocious and irrational as, in the absence of the dialectic, the logic of capital is no longer functional for development; is no longer anything but the power to ensure its own reproduction. The end of dialectic shows clearly that the capitalist function in production is purely parasitic.

Once one goes beyond the dialectical form, is it possible to redefine the form of value as positive, affirmative subjectivity? Or, again, how is the law of surplus value and exploitation displaced, and what new figure can antagonism possibly take?

I do not claim to give here a definitive answer to an open question to which several answers are possible, and only revolutionary practice will have the right to choose between them. I limit myself to identifying the different fields that exercise reflection and to indicating the problematic that I favour.

(a) There are those who argue that the rupture of the dialectical functioning of the law of value leaves as a residue an extremely strong social dualism. Hence the rupture does not imply a shift in the form of value, but underlines the emergence of a position alternative to the development of the law of value and to capitalist command over this development. The end of the dialectic of value liberates use value. And it is from use value that antagonism, self-valorization and exodus arise, as current forms of antagonism.

(b) A second position consists in saying that, once there has been a shift in the constitution of value (apart from the old measures of value), a new dialectic can be set in motion. Just as the rupture ignored the shift in the first position, so in the second the shift avoids the rupture. From this perspective, antagonism appears again as a force that imposes capitalist development or, if you like, the rational management of development by workers. The dialectic can be recovered as a law of historical process, of the progress of labour.

(c) There is a third position in which it seems possible to hold together both the rupture of the dialectical process and the displacement of the production of value. This means that use value has to be reinvented within real subsumption, in its indifference. It means that the displacement of the law of value, following on the collapse of its measure form, is a radical innovation in history. If, in destroying time as a measure, capital imposed the empty verticalization of its power, within this process time and cooperation have nevertheless appeared to be of a common substance. Where use value has definitively disappeared, there necessary labour has become totality. Hence, making real subsumption the new territory of production and of value means positing antagonism as a global collective dimension. From this perspective, antagonism appears as power, as constituent power [*comme puissance, comme pouvoir constituant*]. Exchange value is globally reinvented as use value, in the creativity of new subjects. It is this last revolutionary option that I prefer.

Part II

Workers and Capital Today

4

Marx and Labour*

The Path to Disutopia

There are certainly several utopian conceptions of labour in Marx. I have decided to focus here on only one of them (and not on others that can be found in his works), because it lends itself to a discourse of disutopia: that is, it enables us to grasp in the bud (and to verify today) the transformation of the nature of labour – and therefore to approach a different strategy (different but still within the perspective of communism) for the construction of a subversive subject. A disutopia is a true imagination.

So I shall discuss pages 704–6 of the *Grundrisse*, in the 1993 Penguin translation of Martin Nicolaus.[†] These pages were probably written in April–May 1858, and they make up the central part of the large fragment on the automatic system of machines, which goes from 'Machine' in Notebook VI (p. 690) to the start of Notebook VII (p. 714). I shall focus on pages 704–6, taking them to be the summary and the conclusion of the other pages of the fragment.

We must, moreover, bear in mind – because we shall have to return to this later – that the utopia I am looking at here develops in the middle of a chapter on the circulation of capital; more specifically, it is placed between the distinction between fixed capital and circulating capital and the analysis of the reproduction processes of both. So we are at the heart of the capital system. The title given by the editors to these pages in the French edition ('Fixed capital and the

---

* Originally published as 'Marx et le travail: Le schéma de la désutopie', *Futur antérieur* 35–36 (1996): 189–206.

[†] All page references are to this edition. Toni Negri's original article uses the French translation by Jean-Pierre Lefèbvre (K. Marx, *Manuscrits de 1857–1858 dits Grundrisse (Essentielles)*, Éditions sociales: Paris 2011 [1980]).

development of productive forces') is correct: it is indeed the dynamic and tendential opposition of the two that is here placed centre-stage. The next pages spell out, in two acts and an intermezzo, a real drama-turgy of the struggle between living labour and objectified labour, a dramaturgy that leads us from the analysis of a given contradiction (the crises of the law of value in the tendential development of fixed capital) to the definition of a new subject of production (Intermezzo), and then from the Intermezzo to a displacement (Act Two) in which the new subject is considered a critical actor in the transformation.

One need hardly point out here that the writing of the *Grundrisse* is always guided by the logical movement that takes as its starting point the *Darstellung* [presentation] as a critical description of a relationship or a concept of political economy carried through to its disclosure as crisis; then comes the identification of the new point of view outlined by the opening of the crisis; then the *neue Darstellung* [new presenta-tion] follows – that is, a subversive displacement through which the object or category of political economy has been 'dynamited'. (For more on the functioning of this method, see Antonio Negri, *Marx Beyond Marx: Lessons on the* Grundrisse, Autonomedia: New York, 1991.)

1   Act One

1.1

The exchange of living labour for objectified labour – i.e. the positing of social labour in the form of the contradiction of capital and wage labour – is the ultimate development of the *value-relation* and of production resting on value. Its presupposition is – and remains – the mass of direct labour time, the quantity of labour employed, as the determinant factor in the production of wealth. (704)

Or again, as Marx puts it, the opposition of living labour to objec-tified labour reaches its ultimate form when the exchange between wage labour and capital occurs within a fully deployed social relation-ship. Capitalism has then exhausted (this is the underlying concept) its historical mission of alienating labour and of 'increasing' its pro-ductivity. In the automated system of machines, when fixed capital represents and appropriates the social mass of living labour, the opposition that has dominated the genealogy of capitalist society ceases; labour, presented as immediate labour applied to industry, is no longer the decisive factor in the reproduction of wealth, and therefore the law of value no longer presides over the constitution and regulation of the exchange between labour and capital. Living labour is caught in an insoluble contradiction within the functioning of the dialectical law of value. Here the change is no longer dialectical but rather catastrophic.

The first act of the drama is therefore the last act of the theory of value. *Incipit drama: utopia incipiat* ['The drama begins; let the utopia begin'].

But which utopia is it? Even in Marx, utopia sometimes presents itself as a kind of radical emancipation from the point where the alienated subject had expressed itself – in his words, as the emancipation of that which has always been opposed to capital. In this case, labour is posited as an ineradicable use value in the face of capital, and therefore as a radical opposition to exchange value. 'The real *non-capital* is *labour*' (274). This is not what happens in the pages we are studying here There, in fact, through a different mode of exposition, which is typical of Marx (and which dissipates the ambiguity inherent in the humanist opposition between use value and exchange value), labour as non-capital is analysed not from the point of view of its use but from that of its power [*puissance*]. (On the distinction between the figures of 'labour as non-capital', one grasped negatively – that is, as an existence excluded from wealth, 'as poverty', and therefore as value – and the other grasped positively – that is, as 'living source of value', 'universal possibility of wealth', and *dunamis* – see pp. 295–7.) Consequently, the utopian content of the process is substantially redimensioned: the foreseeable overturning of the law of value does not send living labour back into some indefinite elsewhere, but simply reveals the ultimate effect of its power. I take the liberty of calling this way of imagining the crisis 'disutopia'.

There have been other objections to the description of Marxian research as disutopian. For example, some would discern in the pages we are studying an incontestably teleological dimension: people have spoken of a 'natural history of capital'. However, it seems difficult to take these objections seriously when we consider that, in this Marx here, it is the possible activity, or again the random production of subjectivity, that determines the effectiveness of the structure and development of capital (and also its crisis). This is the method that determines the perspective that embodies the whole materialist tradition of modernity, from Spinoza's *Theological–Political Treatise* to Foucault's chapters on the history of systems of domination, and it would be plainly absurd to call it teleology or naturalism.

But, critics insist, this transcendence of the law of value is considered by Marx to be 'ultimate'! Is this not actually a utopia, they say? It seems possible to reply that here 'ultimate' means only that it is the last obstacle to the revelation of power, and not an absolute limit. And thus an open field of possibilities lies beyond that, still, and always, open to power – unless one thinks that capitalism and the automated system of machines are an irresistible and unsurpassable limit. (I refer the reader to Antonio Negri, *The Savage Anomaly: The Power of Spinoza's Metaphysics and Politics*, trans. Michael Hardt, University of Minnesota Press: Minneapolis, 1991, and to Michael Hardt and Antonio Negri, *Labor of Dionysos*, University of Minnesota Press: Minneapolis, 2007 for clarification of the concept of 'disutopia' [*désutopie*]).

1.2

> But to the degree that large industry develops, the creation of real wealth comes to depend less on labour time and on the amount of labour employed than on the power of the agencies set in motion during labour time, whose 'powerful effectiveness' is itself in turn out of all proportion to the direct labour time spent on their production, but depends rather on the general state of science and on the progress of technology, or the application of this science to production. (The development of this science, especially natural science, and all the others with the latter, is itself in return related to the development of material production.) (704–5)

This passage reads easily. In summary, at the level of large-scale industry, with the introduction of the automated machine system, there is an extraordinary quantitative disproportion between the labour time used and its product, and a qualitative discrepancy between abstract labour and the force of the processes it controls. The law of value effectively presupposed the possibility of quantitatively reducing concrete labour to simple units of abstract labour and of transforming skilled labour (and scientific labour) into a sum of units of abstract labour. The law of value was the effectiveness of this calculation. But here, in the automated system of machines (that is, in large-scale industry at the highest stage of development), quantitative dispersion and qualitative discrepancy 'blow up' any multiplier of units of simple labour.

It follows that, in this form, the law of value goes into crisis. It does not allow the economic calculation of capital; on the contrary, it reveals the political economy of capital as crisis.

On the other hand, new forces of production appear; they are formed by science and technology. Beyond the law of value, then, one will have to define the production of wealth as a result of these new powers and to discover, beyond the 'ultimate contradiction', the emergence of these new powers. 'Real wealth manifests itself, rather – and large industry reveals this – in the monstrous disproportion between the labour time applied, and its product, as well as in the qualitative imbalance between labour, reduced to a pure abstraction, and the power of the production process it superintends' (p. 705).

With this second section we are brought back to the 'ultimate relationship' of 1.1, to the historical process of the crisis of the law of value. This snatches away any possibility of utopia and introduces us into the fabric of power, therefore of disutopia. It establishes the end of the law of value and points to a new path of power.

1.3

Labour no longer appears so much to be included within the production process; rather, the human being comes to relate more as watchman and regulator to the production process itself. (What holds for machinery holds likewise for the combination of human activities and the development of human intercourse.) No longer does the worker insert a modified natural thing as middle link between the object and himself; rather, he inserts the process of nature, transformed into an industrial process, as a means between himself and inorganic nature, mastering it. He steps to the side of the production process instead of being its chief actor. (705)

Once the crisis of the law of value has been established in the form of quantitative disproportion and qualitative discrepancy, and once the appearance of new forces of production, science and technology has been determined, it remains to show in what respect the position of the worker in the new machine system is now different and what it is that defines this difference. So, Marx tells us, immediate labour power, be it individual or collective or both, is located alongside the process of production, itself grasped in its immediate form. The worker becomes the supervisor or regulator of the automated and continuous process of production. Labour presents itself as a partly conscious organ, a living accessory to the great automated organization of machines.

We can say, then, that the dialectic of the tool of labour, of this tool of labour that workers inserted as a mediator between themselves and inorganic nature, is over. 'It is the machine . . . which is itself the virtuoso' (693). 'The worker appears as superfluous' (695). The machine absorbed the tool and recreated the worker as a function proper to itself.

We shall examine later the note that Marx introduces, in brackets, in the passage I have looked at: he says there that what is true of machinery is also true of the combination of human activities and the development of trade among human beings. This means that human society too, in its collective form, presents itself as an industrial process – the natural form of the capitalist enterprise characterized by the automated machine.

Pages 692–3 definitively illustrate the image of the new automated process of big industry, in which the function of the law of value (in its traditional form) and the conception of direct labour (as the main force of production) are reduced to zero.

> [In mechanized production], the appropriation of living labour by objectified labour – of the power or activity which creates value by value existing for itself – which lies in the concept of capital, is posited, in production resting on machinery, as the character of the production process itself, including its material elements and its material motion. The production process has ceased to be a labour process in the sense of a process dominated by labour as its governing unity. (693)

With this, Act One comes to a close. The law of value and the function of valorization of immediate (individual and collective) labour have been expounded in critical form. 'In critical form' in this case means that the very dialectic of the capitalist relation of exploitation runs the risk of being interrupted. The worker is no longer essential to the production of value or to the building of wealth.

Who is responsible for the production of value and wealth?

2 Intermezzo

> In this transformation, it is neither the direct human labour he himself performs, nor the time during which he works, but rather the appropriation of his own general productive power, his understanding of nature and his mastery over it by virtue of his presence as a social body – it is, in a word, the development of the social individual which appears as the great foundation-stone of production and wealth. (705)

The mutation lies in the transformation of the mode of appropriation of productivity by capital. The main element in the production of value and wealth is no longer direct labour, but this general productive force that arises from the social body of knowing and doing; the fundamental pillar of production and wealth is the social individual.

This mutation has already been pointed out: 'The accumulation of knowledge and of skill, of the general productive forces of the social brain is thus absorbed into capital, as opposed to labour' (p. 694).

But the mutation was signalled only from an objective point of view. Also, still from an objective point of view, it was stressed that this new aspect of the capital relation (the appropriation of scientific and social productivity in general) was more visible in the figure of circulating capital than in that of fixed capital. Hence, again, the objective point of view, even rendered mobile and dynamic.

However, for a real reversal to be given, something more is needed: the definition of a new subject of production. Once the social individual has become the pillar of wealth, theory must make that social individual appear as the creator of that wealth. This is the direction taken by Marx's analysis.

Now, immediate labour remains essential but becomes subaltern in the process of valorization by comparison with scientific production, the application of technologies, and so on, and this essentially depends on the development of labour cooperation and its rooting at the subjective level. This cooperative force that constitutes the 'natural fruit of social labour' (700) is expressed and transcended in social labour. We see here the replacement of direct labour by social labour (700). Production based on science and technology is above all based on this 'general productive force arising from social combination [*Gliederung*] in total production on the other side – a combination which appears as a natural fruit of social labour (although it is a historic product). Capital thus works towards its own dissolution as the form dominating production' (700). The new subjective form of the social (scientific, technological) individual who produces value is also highlighted (immediately after pp. 706–7), and always in the same terms: while direct labour ceases to be the basis of production, the 'combination' of social activities – which big industry itself has built, and which in this transformation conquers its own subjectivity – is becoming more and more marked.

Having arrived at this transformation, we find ourselves brought directly back to the positive definition of labour and non-capital, as referenced in 1.1 (see pp. 295–6). The power of non-capital, the power of labour, resides – I mean, is determined – here, in its social creativity, or (if you like) in its constituent power. This sociality was imposed in simple cooperation: it is in the process of its recognition that individuals engage in this production of subjectivity, which is self-recognition as a class. It is, then, at this moment that a new ontological arrangement of subjectivation is imposed at this new level of development, when the instrument of labour is at the same time completely expropriated by capital and completely reappropriated in the intellectual nature of labour.

Here open two chapters that need to be addressed separately and that I have addressed in part in *Marx beyond Marx*.

The first concerns the processes of mediation (*Vergleichung*) internal to the movement of transforming labour power from immediacy into intellectual and scientific mediation. The theme is introduced according to a scheme that undoubtedly remains fairly objectivist: that of the mobilization of the labour value in circulation.

The second problem is much broader: it consists in fixing the relations that link the modification of the technical composition of labour power to the new ontological determinations it assumes in the development of capitalism; therefore it consists in fixing within this dialectic the different figures of production of subjectivity. In short, this is about defining an ontology of the historical development of class figures. This is where the second act of Marx's research begins.

3   Act Two

3.1

The *theft of alien labour time, on which the present wealth is based*, appears a miserable foundation in face of this new one, created by large-scale industry itself. As soon as labour in the direct form has ceased to be the great well-spring of wealth, labour time ceases and must cease to be its measure, and hence exchange value [must cease to be the measure] of use value. The *surplus labour of the mass* has ceased to be the condition for the development of general wealth, just as the *non-labour of the few*, for the development of the general powers of the human head. With that, production based on exchange value breaks down, and the direct, material production process is stripped of the form of penury and antithesis. The free development of individualities, and hence not the reduction of necessary labour time so as to posit surplus labour, but rather the general reduction of the necessary labour of society to a minimum, which then corresponds to the artistic, scientific etc. development of the individuals in the time set free, and with the means created, for all of them. (705–6)

The analysis (*Darstellung*) and the identification of the new subject are now followed by the subversive displacement, that is to say the *neue Darstellung*.

In this first transition to the *neue Darstellung* one can highlight four points, closely linked among themselves and articulated by a disutopian political project that begins to take shape. Marx here takes up subversively what thus far he has developed in analytical terms.

(a) The ending of the operation of the law of value in its classic form makes explicit what the law of value has always been: a law of exploitation. The law of value does not exist, there is only a law of surplus value. In capitalist development, the law of value finds a mystified application, but only at the price of its cancellation.

(b) The classic capitalist conditions for the production of wealth are in crisis. The transformation of living labour (beyond immediate labour) into intellectual or immaterial labour, a producer of artistic, scientific and technical functions that may be cooperative, social and linguistic – well, this transformation is not only possible but actual: it is taking place before our eyes.

(c) The crisis of the law of value means that labour no longer appears in the form of poverty. As an activity, as an ontological potentiality, living labour becomes a (socially) direct producer of wealth.

(d) Necessary labour is no longer the condition of surplus labour. The reduction in necessary labour has indeed reached a minimum that has nothing to do with the wealth produced; in other words there is no possible common measure between them any more. Necessary labour reaches a limit that is rather proportional with an immense productivity, but of another nature than that determined by direct labour: scientific production, artistic expression, free social time as productive *dunamis*.

The reduction of necessary labour, through a massive increase in productivity, to a decreasing minimum effectively frees up time available to the whole of society. Capital no longer succeeds in transforming this available free time into surplus value or in chaining it to its growth. The time available therefore ceases to exist in a contradictory way (that is, ceases to be able to exist only on the basis of surplus labour). Real wealth presents itself as a product of the activity of all individuals, and the available time is from now on the measure of wealth.

On this subject one reads:

The more this contradiction develops, the more does it become evident that the growth of the forces of production can no longer be bound up with the appropriation of alien labour, but that the mass of workers must themselves appropriate their own surplus labour. Once they have done so – and *disposable time* thereby ceases to have an *antithetical* existence – then, on the one side, necessary labour time will be measured by the needs of the social individual, and, on the other, the development of the power of social production will grow so rapidly that, even though production is now calculated for the wealth of all, *disposable time* will grow for all. For real wealth is the developed productive power of all individuals. The measure of wealth is then not any longer, in any way, labour time, but rather disposable time. (708)

3.2

Capital itself is the moving contradiction, [in] that it presses to reduce labour time to a minimum, while it posits labour time, on the other side, as sole measure and source of wealth. Hence it diminishes labour time in the necessary form so as to increase it in the superfluous form; hence posits the superfluous in growing measure as a condition – question of life or death – for the necessary. On the one side, then, it calls to life all the powers of science and of nature, as of social combination and of social intercourse, in order to make the creation of wealth independent (relatively) of the labour time employed on it. On the other side, it wants to use labour-time as the measuring rod for the giant social forces thereby created, and to confine them within the limits required to maintain the already created value as value. Forces of production and social relations – two different sides of the development of the social individual – appear to capital as mere means, and are merely means for it to produce on its limited foundation. In fact, however, they are the material conditions to blow this foundation sky-high. 'Truly wealthy a nation, when the working day is 6 rather than 12 hours. *Wealth* is not command over surplus labour time' (real wealth), 'but rather *disposable time* outside that needed in direct production, for *every individual* and the whole society' (*The Source and Remedy* etc. 1821, p. 6). (706)

Once this situation has come about – and it is capital itself that has produced it (but we know that developments of capital are also, invariably, the result of class struggle) – once this situation has come about, what issues are at stake for class struggle?

From a capitalist point of view, the question is to impose the measurement of the law of value – that is, the temporal measurement of the exploitation of immediate labour – by countering the transformation of the subjects of labour and of production. This is a matter of life or death. Capital can live only from the law of direct labour. Its mode of organization is based on this figure of alienation. Capital is unable to move beyond the limits of its base.

The paradox that surfaces here can be defined as follows: on the one hand, the powers of science and communication, which have become really and immediately productive, emancipate themselves from the law of value, that is, from the coercive measure of immediate labour time [*temps de travail immédiat*] On the other hand, the intangible force of production and productive social relations (communication) – these two complementary sides of the development of the social individual – must be reduced within the narrow base of the law of value. But, that being so, capital and its power no longer have any rationality. The production of goods is carried out through command – not through labour, not through goods, only through command. This brings us back to the situation that Marx defined at the beginning of the summary and exposition of the crisis of the law of value (quoted in section 1.1 here): but now the historical process, which has matured through the transformation of the subject, comes in a form that is contradictory in terms of subjectivity.

'Disutopia' has come of age. The process has reached the point where new subjective forms have to 'explode' the old system of the law of value, of the law of exploitation. From the point of view of the new proletariat, of the new figures of living labour, the class struggle is played out in the organization of the new powers of production against capitalist domination.

3.3

Nature builds no machines, no locomotives, railways, electric telegraphs, self-acting mules etc. These are products of human industry; natural material transformed into organs of the human will over nature, or of human participation in nature. They are *organs of the human brain, created by the human hand*; the power of knowledge, objectified. The development of fixed capital indicates to what degree general social knowledge has become a *direct force of production*, and to what degree, hence, the conditions of the process of social life itself have come under the control of the general intellect and been transformed in accordance with it. To what degree the powers of social production have been produced, not only in the form of knowledge, but also as immediate organs of social practice, of the real life process. (706)

Marx's final proposal concerns the content of class struggle seen from the point of view of the new, scientific–communicational proletariat. The new social labour power has to impose its own hegemony on the general intellect.

If you look closely, the project is by no means scientistic *à la* Saint-Simon. It is, by and large, a social project. It is social practice that constitutes value, it is the real process of life that nourishes it. There is no trace of economism in this conception of proletarian overthrow of capitalist domination (but we know what this 'new' proletariat is!). The nature of the new intellectual–immaterial labour power is outlined here. Marx shows us its characteristics:

(a) But obviously this process of inversion is a merely *historical* necessity, a necessity for the development of the forces of production solely from a specific historic point of departure, or basis, but in no way an *absolute* necessity of production; rather, a vanishing one, and the result and inherent purpose of this process is to suspend this basis itself, together with this form of the process. The bourgeois economists are so much cooped up within the notions belonging to a specific historic stage of social development that the necessity of the *objectification* of the powers of social labour appear to them as inseparable from the necessity of their *alienation vis-à-vis* living labour. But with the suspension of the *immediate* character of living labour, as merely *individual*, or as general merely internally or merely externally, with the positing of the activity of individuals as immediately general or *social* activity, the objective moments of production are stripped of this form of alienation; they are thereby posited as property, as the organic social body within which the individuals reproduce themselves as individuals, but as social individuals. The conditions which allow them to exist in this way in the reproduction of their life, in their productive life's process, have been posited only by the historic economic process itself; both the objective and the subjective conditions, which are only the two distinct forms of the same conditions. (832)

(b) And then:
Real saving – economy – = saving of labour time = development of productive force. Suspension of the contradiction between free time and labour time. – True conception of the process of social production

Real economy – saving – consists of the saving of labour time (minimum (and minimization) of production costs); but this saving identical with development of the productive force. Hence in no way *abstinence from consumption*, but rather the development of power, of capabilities of production, and hence both of the capabilities as well as the means of consumption. The capability to consume is a condition of consumption, hence its primary means, and this capability is the development of an individual potential, a force of production. The saving of labour time [is] equal to an increase of free time, i.e. time for the full development of the individual, which in turn reacts back upon the productive power of labour as itself the greatest productive power. From the standpoint of the direct production process it can be regarded as the production of *fixed capital*, this fixed capital being man himself. It goes without saying, by the way, that direct labour time itself cannot remain in the abstract antithesis to free time in which it appears from the perspective of bourgeois economy. Labour cannot become play, as Fourier would like, although it remains his great contribution to have expressed the suspension not of distribution, but of the mode of production itself, in a higher form, as the ultimate object. Free time – which is both idle time and time for higher activity – has naturally transformed its possessor into a different subject, and he then enters into the direct production process as this different subject The process is then both discipline, as regards the human being in the process of becoming; and, at the same time, practice [*Ausübung*], experimental science, materially creative and objectifying science, as regards the human being who has become, in whose head exists the accumulated knowledge of society. For both, in so far as labour requires practical use of the hands and free bodily movement, as in agriculture, at the same time exercise. (711–12)

As the system of bourgeois economy has developed for us only by degrees, so too its negation, which is its ultimate result. We are still concerned now with the direct production process. When we consider bourgeois society in the long view and as a whole, then the final result of the process of social production always appears as the society itself, i.e. the human being itself in its social relations. Everything that has a fixed form, such as the product etc., appears as merely a moment, a vanishing moment, in this movement. The direct production process itself here appears only as a moment. The conditions and objectifications of the process are themselves equally moments of it, and its only subjects are the individuals, but individuals in mutual relationships, which they equally reproduce and produce anew. The constant process of their own movement, in which they renew themselves even as they renew the world of wealth they create. (712)

4 The history of an interpretation and of its developments

The content of Marx's utopia of labour – in the context in which we have looked at it – consists in highlighting the tendency to productive hegemony of social knowledge-power (a knowledge-power that is intellectual and cooperative) and in making it its calling to destroy rather than orient the development of capitalistic society and to build a society of rich and cooperating individualities.

One can find in Marx's oeuvre other utopias of associated labour and communism. But the one to which I grew most attached seems to me particularly strong. It is similar in design to other utopian approaches; indeed, it has a new ontological dimension, which is linked to the transformation of labour, and therefore of humanity, from a natural productive being into an intellectual and social productive being. The analysis of the anthropological mutation introduces in the utopian perspective a realist dimension that eliminates its idealist features and subjects the relation between reality and rationality (*Wirklichkeit und Rationalität*) to an immanent genealogy. This is when utopia becomes disutopia.

The realism of the Marxian disutopia under scrutiny here is confirmed today by the experience of labour transformations in postmodern postindustrial societies. But this discovery would be irrelevant and even ambiguous if it had not been brought about through a rigorous and coherent application of genealogical method, of the immanence of the field, and by putting it into perspective with the production of subjectivity: these are among the most topical categories in contemporary thought, but were already set to work by Marx. *Experientia sive praxis* [experience or praxis].

This richness of Marx's disutopia has gradually revealed itself in the development of the class struggle and essentially in the second half of the twentieth century. It corresponds, if I may say so, to the great transformation of labour and capitalism marked by 1968.

Speaking from direct knowledge, I shall briefly enumerate here the successive phases of reading this text in the extraordinary laboratory of revolutionary experience that was Italy in the 1960s and 1970s.

(a) In 1960 the 'Fragment on Machines' was translated by Renato Solmi and published by *Quaderni Rossi*. Panzieri gave it a first reading, essentially in Frankfurt School style – as a critique of machinery and as an interpretation of fixed capital as domination.

(b) In the years 1962–4, a reading of the 'Fragment' was produced in the journal *Classe operaia* that accentuated the dualism and the antagonism between labour power (living labour) and fixed capital (objectified labour) and attempted to build an inverted articulation of their relationship. The fundamental thesis was that the development of labour power anticipates and foreshadows that of fixed capital. Alquati and Tronti developed this reading further.

(c) In 1967–8 the 'Fragment' was used as a means of consolidating the Marxian theory of crises. In reality it served to articulate the objectivist definitions of the crisis (crisis of proportion and crisis of overproduction) from a subjective point of view: the crisis as a product of the structural transformation of the proletarian subject. From this perspective, one could begin to read 1968 in terms of a revolution in the concept of labour power and of a genealogy and hegemony of immaterial labour.

(d) From 1973 to 1978 (in particular in my 'Marx beyond Marx' lectures) people were reading the 'Fragment' as a central element in the dynamics of interpretation of the transformations of the class subject, and hence (a) as a theory of ontological displacement and (b) as the genesis of the 'social worker' [*operaio sociale*] (first definition of the crisis of direct labour and of the recomposition of the new and cooperative revolutionary subject). Interest at that time was focused mainly on the ontological dimension of displacement, on emphasizing the intensity of the force of the historical transformation.

(e) Finally, from the mid-1980s on, the reading interest came to focus on the phenomenology and sociology of intellectual labour, in other words of the new immaterial labour power, which capitalist development and the class struggle were placing at the centre of the analysis. The new determination of living labour is manifested in the case of political hegemony, which it directs towards general intellect – for the revolutionary overturning of its concept.

The problem of exploitation (of immaterial labour) is once again placed at the heart of the analysis.

And it is with this task in mind that I can sign off (give up – me?): the analysis of the new nature of labour, viewed from the perspective of its communist revolution. This is the hypothesis that we inherit from Marx's *Fragment* of 1858 . . .

5

The Capital–Labour Relationship in Cognitive Capitalism*

Antonio Negri and Carlo Vercellone

In the transition from industrial capitalism to cognitive capitalism, the capital–labour relationship is marked by a radical transformation. This involves three inseparable elements: the mode of production; the class composition, on which the valorization of capital rests; and, finally, the forms of distribution of income between wages, rent and profit. The intention of this chapter is to reconstruct the basic characteristics of this great transformation and the stakes involved. In doing this, we shall proceed in three stages. After recalling the origin and historical direction of the process that has led to the hegemony of cognitive labour, we shall analyse the main characteristics that allow us to define the current transformation of the capital–labour relation. We shall end by showing why the increasingly central role of rent displaces the terms of the traditional antagonism, which is based on the opposition between wages and company profits.

1 From the mass worker to the hegemony of cognitive labour

Today we witness a change of the capital–labour relationship that runs in an opposite direction to the one studied by Gramsci in *Americanism and Fordism* in the 1930s but is comparable to it in importance. To understand the origin and scope of this historic turn-

* Originally published under the title 'Il rapporto capitale/lavoro nel capitalismo cognitivo', in *Posse* (October 2007): 46–56, https://halshs.archives-ouvertes.fr/halshs-00264147/document; French translation 'Le rapport capital/travail dans le capitalisme cognitif', in *Multitudes* 32 (2008): 39–50.

ing point, we should remember that, during the postwar period, Fordist growth represented the fulfilment of the logic of development of an industrial capitalism that was founded on four main tendencies: the social polarization of knowledges [*saperi*] and the separation of intellectual work from manual work; the hegemony of knowledges [*conoscenze*] incorporated in fixed assets and the managerial organization of enterprises; the centrality of material labour, which was subjected to Taylorist norms of extraction of surplus value; and the strategic role of fixed capital as the principal form of property and technological progress.

After the crisis of Fordism, these trends came into question. The starting point of the upheaval lay in the conflictual dynamics through which the mass worker had destructured the foundations of the scientific organization of work and had led to a formidable expansion of the guarantees and collective services of welfare, far beyond what was compatible with Fordism. The result was a weakening of the monetary constraint on the wage relation and a strong process of collective reappropriation of the intellectual powers [*potenze*] of production.

It was through this antagonistic dynamic that the mass worker brought about the structural crisis of the Fordist model, while constructing, at the very heart of capital, the elements of a common [*un comune*] and of an ontological transformation of labour that looked beyond the logic of capital. The factory working class had negated itself (or at least its centrality) by constructing the figure of the collective worker of general intellect* and the subjective conditions, as well as the structural forms, of an economy based on the motor role and the diffusion of knowledge. The result was the opening of a new historical phase in the capital–labour relation, one marked by a complete return of the cognitive dimension of labour and by the construction of a diffuse intellectuality.

Two essential points need to be underlined for a correct characterization of the genesis and nature of the new capitalism.

The first is that the essential motor of the emergence of a knowledge-based economy resides in the power of living labour. The formation of a knowledge-based economy precedes and opposes, both logically and historically, the genesis of cognitive capitalism. The latter is in fact the result of a restructuring process through which capital tries to absorb and parasitically subjugate the collective conditions of knowledge production, stifling the potential for emancipation

---

* 'General intellect' in English in the original thoughout this chapter.

inscribed in the society of general intellect. Thus, when we use the concept of cognitive capitalism, we refer to a system of accumulation in which the productive value of intellectual and immaterial labour becomes dominant and where the central axis of capital's valorization relates directly to the expropriation of the common 'through rent' [*'attraverso la rendita'*] and to the transformation of knowledge into a commodity.

The second point is that, contrary to the claims of theorists of the information revolution, the determining element of the current transformation of labour cannot be explained by appeal to a technological determinism based on the driving role of information and communication technologies (ICTs). In fact these theories forget two essential elements: ICTs are able to function correctly only thanks to a living knowledge capable of mobilizing them, since it is this knowledge that governs the processing of information; without it information would be a sterile resource, as is capital without labour. So the main creative force of the ICT revolution does not derive from a dynamic driven by capital; it relies on the creation of social networks for cooperation in the labour process, networks that herald forms of organization that are alternative both to the business model and to the market, as forms of coordination of production.

2   The main characteristics of the new capital–labour relationship

The growth in power of the cognitive aspect of work corresponds to the affirmation of a new hegemony of knowledges [*conoscenze*], mobilized by labour, in relation to the knowledges [*saperi*] incorporated in fixed assets and in the managerial organization of companies. Even more, it is now living labour that carries out a large number of the main functions once performed by fixed capital. Knowledge is increasingly collectively shared, and this fact radically changes both the internal organization of companies and their relationship with the outside. In the new figure of the capital–labour relationship, as we shall see, labour is thus within the enterprise but at the same time gets organized outside it.

In this evolution, the set of Fordist–industrial conventions associated with the wage relation, the notion of productive labour, the measure of value, the forms of property and the distribution of income are profoundly altered. We indicate below some of the motifs [*stilemi*] that characterize the extent of this transformation.

2.1 The overturning of the relationship between living and dead labour and between factory and society

The first motif refers to the historical dynamic through which that part of capital known as intangible – R&D [research and development] and especially education, training and health, which are essentially incorporated in human beings (what is often and wrongly called human capital) – has exceeded the share of material capital in the real stock of capital and has become the main factor of growth. Consequently this trend is closely linked to factors that underlie the emergence of a diffuse intellectuality – which explains the increasingly significant part played by the capital labeled 'intangible'.

More precisely, the interpretation of this motif has at least four major meanings, which are almost systematically concealed by OECD economists.

The first is that, contrary to an idea conveyed by knowledge-based economy* economists, the social conditions and the real, driving sectors of an economy based on knowledge are not found in private R&D laboratories. On the contrary, they correspond to the collective productions of people and for people [*produzioni collettive dell'uomo e per l'uomo*], which are traditionally guaranteed by the common institutions of the welfare state† (health, education, public and university research, and the like). This element is systematically omitted by economists at the OECD, precisely at a time when we are seeing an extraordinary pressure to privatize these institutions. The explanation for this gross concealment is linked to the strategic role that biopolitical control and the mercantile colonization of welfare institutions play for cognitive capital. Healthcare, education, training and culture are not only growing sectors of production but, even more, they form people's ways of life. And this opens the terrain for a central conflict between the neoliberal strategies of privatization of the common and the projects of democratic reappropriation of the institution of welfare.

The second meaning of this motif is that now it is labour that performs certain essential functions traditionally guaranteed by constant capital, both in terms of production organization and as the main factor of competitiveness and advance in knowledges. Christian Marazzi has clearly highlighted this aspect.

---

* 'Knowledge-based economy' in English in the original.
† 'Welfare state' in English in the original throughout this chapter.

The third meaning lies in the fact that the conditions of the formation and reproduction of labour power are now directly productive, and that therefore the source of the 'wealth of nations' today increasingly resides in a cooperation located upstream from the walls of the enterprises. We might also note that, in the light of these developments, the canonical model of the theory of knowledge (according to which the production of knowledge is the prerogative of an elite section of the workforce, a sector that specializes in this function) loses all meaning. This sector – if one can still use this term – actually corresponds to the whole of society today. As a result, the very concept of productive labour needs to be extended to the totality of social times that take part in economic and social production and reproduction.

Finally, the so-called higher services, historically guaranteed by the welfare state, can be seen as activities in which the cognitive, communicative and affective dimension of labour is dominant and where it would be possible to develop radically new forms of self-management of labour, forms based on a co-production of services that closely involves the users.

2.2 Cognitive division of labour, working class, and destabilization of the canonical terms of the wage relation

The second motif is the passage from a Taylorist division of labour to a cognitive division of labour. In this context, production efficiency no longer relies on the reduction of the operating time required for each task, but is based on the knowledge and versatility of a workforce capable of maximizing its aptitude for learning, innovation and adaptation to a dynamic of continuous change.

We note that, beyond the paradigmatic model of the higher services and the high-tech activities of the new economy, the diffusion of activities of knowledge production and information processing applies to all economic sectors, including those with low technological intensity. This is indicated by the generalized tendency towards self-employment in work.

Of course, this trend is not univocal. Within a given single sector, certain phases of the production process can be organized in accordance with cognitive principles, while other stages of production (especially the more standardized industrial operations) can continue to be based on a Taylorist or neo-Taylorist type of labour. Nonetheless, both qualitatively and quantitatively, it is cognitive labour that is at the centre of the process of capital valorization, at least in OECD countries, and that in consequence has the power possibly to break with the mechanisms of capitalist production.

From this point of view it should be emphasized, and here is the third motif, that the growth of the cognitive dimension of work induces a double destabilization of the canonical principles that regulate the capital–labour exchange.

On the one hand, in in knowledge-intensive activities, when the product of labour takes an eminently immaterial form, we witness how one of the primary conditions of the wage contract is called into question: this is the workers' waiver (in exchange for the wage) of any claim over the ownership of the product of their labour. In activities such as research or software production, labour does not crystallize into a material product that is separate from the worker: it remains embedded in the workers' brains, and is therefore inseparable from their persons. Among other things, this contributes to explaining the pressure exerted by companies to obtain a transformation and a strengthening of intellectual property rights, in order to be able to appropriate knowledge and control the mechanisms that permit its circulation.

On the other hand, the precise delimitation and synchronization of time and place that structured the Fordist norm of the wage contract are profoundly changed today. Why is this? In the energy paradigm of industrial capitalism, the payment of wages signalled the purchase by capital of a precisely defined fraction of human time that was made available to companies. Within the framework of this time for work, the employer had to take charge of finding the most effective ways to use that paid time, in order to wrest from the use value of labour power the greatest possible amount of surplus labour. Obviously all this did not happen spontaneously, since by their nature capital and labour have essentially contradictory interests. The principles of a scientific organization of work – through the expropriation of working-class knowledge and a rigid imposition of times and tasks – constituted for a period an adequate answer to this decisive question.

But everything changes when labour, in the process of becoming increasingly immaterial and cognitive, can no longer be reduced to a simple consumption of energy carried out in a given time. The old dilemma of control over labour reappears in new forms. Capital not only has become dependent on the knowledge of waged workers but must obtain a mobilization and an active involvement of the totality of knowledges and lifetimes of waged workers.

The prescription of subjectivity for the purpose of obtaining an internalization of the objectives of the company, the drive for results, and a responsiveness to customer pressure, together with the constraint linked, plain and simple, to precarity, are the main ways found by capital to try to respond to this new problem. The various forms of precarization of work are actually in the first place a tool for capital to impose this total subordination and to benefit from it for free, without recognizing and without paying the wages that correspond to this time, which is not integrated into and is not measurable by the employment contract. These developments translate into an increase in work that is not measured and is difficult to quantify according to the traditional criteria of work measurement. This is one of the elements that must lead us to an overall rethinking of the notion of time of productive labour and the notion of wage by comparison with the Fordist era.

This is also one of the key explanations of the observation that, in knowledge capitalism, precarity plays a similar role in the organization of labour to the role played by the Taylorist fragmentation of jobs in industrial capitalism.

The same logic explains why the process of de-skilling the workforce appears to have now given way to a massive downgrading phenomenon – which affects especially women and young graduates – that is, a devaluation of remuneration and employment conditions in relation to the actual skills used in carrying out the work activity.

3   The crisis of the threefold formula: The rent economy and the privatization of the common

The transformations in the mode of production are closely associated with a major transformation in the forms of capture of surplus value and distribution of income. In this context, two major changes need to be studied.

The first concerns the manifest gap between the increasingly social nature of production and the mechanisms of wage formation: the latter remain prisoners to the old Fordist rules that make access to income dependent on employment. This gap has contributed strongly to the stagnation of real wages and to the precarization of living conditions. At the same time, there has been a drastic reduction in the amount and the beneficiaries of social benefits that are based on objective rights (linked to social contributions or citizenship rights). The outcome of this is a transition from the welfare system to a workfare state* system, in which the priority accorded to welfare services that offer very low amounts of money and are subjected to a strong set of conditions stigmatizes the beneficiaries and weakens the bargaining power of the whole work force.

The second development concerns the vigorous return of rent. Rent is seen as the principal tool, both for the capture of surplus value and for desocializing the common. The meaning and the key role of this development of rent can be understood at two main levels.

On the one hand, at the level of the social organization of production, the very criteria of the traditional distinction between income and profit become less and less pertinent. This blurring of the borders between rent and profit finds one of its expressions in the way in which financial power reshapes the criteria of governance† of enterprises, having regard only for the creation of value for the shareholder. Everything happens as if the movement of the autonomization of the cooperation of labour is matched by a parallel movement of autonomization of capital in the abstract, flexible and mobile form of capital money [*capitale-denaro*]. This is a new qualitative leap related to the historical process that had led to a growing separation between the management and the ownership of capital. Why does this happen? It happens because the era of cognitive capitalism not only sees the definitive decline of the idyllic figure of the Weberian entrepreneur (who combined in one person the functions of ownership and company management); even more, it coincides with the irreversible crisis of the Galbraithian technostructure, which draws its legitimacy from the role that innovation played in programming and from the role that work played in the organization. These figures give way to the figure of a management‡ whose main expertise lies in the exercise of financial and speculative functions, while – as we have seen – the actual functions of production organization are increasingly attributed to the employee. This evolution can be noted at the level of individual companies (here you could speak of absolute rent), and also at the level of relationships between business and society. Indeed, the competitiveness of companies depends more and more not on internal economies but on external economies, in other words on the ability to capture the productive surpluses that come from the cognitive resources of a given territory. This is, on an unprecedented

---

* 'Workfare state' is in English in the original.
† 'Governance' is in English in the original.
‡ 'Management' is in English in the original.

historical scale, what Marshall qualified as rent, in order to distinguish clearly this 'free gift', which results 'from the general progress of society', from the normal sources of profit. In short, capital acquires the benefits of the collective knowledge of society free of charge, as if it were a gift of nature, and this part of the surplus value is comparable point by point with the differential rent from which the owners of the most fertile lands benefit.

On the other hand the current development of rent corresponds to its purer shapes and functions, those that had laid the foundation of the genesis of capitalism through the experience of the enclosures.* In this respect, rent appears as the product of a privatization of the common that makes it possible, on this basis, to draw an income generated by the creation of an artificial scarcity of resources. This is the common element that brings together, in a single logic, the income from real estate speculation and the financial rent that, since the early 1980s, thanks to the privatization of money and public debt, has played a growing role in fiscal crisis and the dismantling of the institutions of the welfare state. A similar logic presides over the attempt to privatize knowledge and the living, thanks to a policy of strengthening intellectual property rights that makes it possible for the costs of numerous commodities to be kept artificially high, whereas their reproduction costs are extremely low or even approaching zero. We have here a further manifestation of the crisis of the law of value and of the antagonism between capital and labour in the era of general intellect.

These profound changes in the relationships between wage, rent and profit are also the pivot of a policy of segmentation of class composition and of the labour market towards a strongly dualistic configuration.

A first sector comprises a privileged minority of labour power, used in activities that are the most profitable and often the most parasitic ones in cognitive capitalism, such as the provision of financial services to companies, research oriented towards obtaining patents, and specialist legal activities in the defence of intellectual property rights. This component of the so-called cognitariat (which could also be described as 'functionaries of capital's rent') has its qualifications and competences explicitly recognized Besides, these workers increasingly find in their 'pay packets' a share of the dividends of finance capital, as well as benefitting from forms of protection linked to a

---

* 'Enclosures' is in English in the original.

system of pension funds and private insurance. The second sector, on the other hand, comprises a workforce whose qualifications and skills are not recognized. Thus, as we have seen, this majority category of cognitive labour ends up suffering a heavy process of downgrading [*declassamento*]. This sector must cover and ensure not only the most precarious jobs in the new cognitive division of labour, but also the neo-Taylorist functions of the new standardized services, which are linked to the development of low-wage personal services. The dualism of the labour market and the distribution of income thus reinforces, in a vicious circle, the dismantling of collective welfare services to the benefit of the expansion of commercial services to the people who are at the base of contemporary domesticity.

In short, rent, in its different forms (financial, real estate, cognitive, waged etc.), occupies an increasingly strategic space in income distribution and in the social stratification of the population. The result is the disintegration of what we used to call 'the middle classes' and the creation of an 'hourglass society', marked by an extreme polarization of wealth – unless capital is forced to concede to labour a growing autonomy in the organization of production – and this is the only reformist option that it is possible to imagine in the short term, bearing in mind that the principal source of value resides now in the creativity, polyvalence and invention power of waged workers, and not in fixed capital and in the customary work of execution. In effect capital is already doing this; but it limits this autonomy to the choice of ways of reaching objectives that are hetero-determined. The political problem is how to take this power away from capital, and hence how to propose, autonomously, new institutions of the common. The democratic reconquest of the institution of welfare, which is based on the dynamics of association and on the self-organization of labour that currently traverses society, thus appears – from the point of view of norms both of production and of consumption – as a determining element in the construction of an alternative model of development: a model based on the priority of the production of human beings for and through human beings [*produzione dell'uomo per e attraverso l'uomo*] When, in the production of general intellect, the principal fixed capital becomes human beings themselves, then, with this concept, one has to understand a logic of social cooperation that is situated beyond the law of value and beyond the threefold formula itself. It is within such a perspective that we can locate the struggle for the establishment of an unconditional guaranteed social income [*reddito sociale garantito*] conceived of as a primary income – in other words, tied not to distribution (like a *revenu minimum d'insertion*

[RMI]) but to the affirmation of the increasingly collective character of the production of value and wealth. That would permit the recomposition and strengthening of the contractual power of the whole labour force, removing from capital a part of the value captured by rent. At the same time, the weakening of the monetary constraint on the wage relation would favour the development of forms of labour emancipated from mercantile logic and from subordinated labour.

6

The Organic Composition of Capital Today*

1. In the debate on the impact of digital technologies on society, bearing in mind that these technologies have profoundly changed the 'mode of production' (apart from our ways of knowing and communicating), people have advanced the solid hypothesis that the worker, the producer, has been transformed by the use of the digital machine. The discussion concerning the psycho-political consequences of digital machinery is so broad-ranging that I can only mention it here, even if the conclusions that these researches produce are highly problematic. They usually draw conclusions about a passive subjection of the worker to the machine, and a generalized alienation, and an epidemic of depressive illnesses, and a definition of algorithmic Taylorisms, and the list goes on and on. In these doom-laden predictions we hear the old Nazi adage blowing: 'the earth now reveals itself as a coal mining district' and affects humans in their essence.[1] Arguably it would be more sophisticated to think about the impact of digital technology by asking ourselves whether, and also how, the bodies and minds of the workers might take possession of the digital machine – and quietly to remind ourselves that, although the new impact of the digital machine on the producer takes place under the command of capital, the producer not only yields value to the constant capital during the production process: qua labour power, both in its singular productive contribution and in its cooperative use of the digital machine, the

* Paper first published in 2017 in EuroNomade, as 'Appropriazione di capitale fisso: Una metafora?', http://www.euronomade.info/?p=8936, then presented at the École Normale Supérieure d'Ulm, 5 February 2018.

producer also connects to the machine and can become one with it when the connection takes place in the immaterial flow of cognitive labour. In cognitive labour, living labour, although submitted to fixed capital when it develops its productive capacity, can invest it (i.e. fixed capital), being simultaneously its active matter and its engine. Consequently, in Marxist circles, one talks now of an 'appropriation of fixed capital' by the digital worker, the cognitive producer. When one analyses the increased productivity of digital operators or the productive capacities of these 'digital natives', these issues and problems come up spontaneously. Are they simple metaphors?

2.   And, more to the point, are they simple political metaphors? In talking about an 'appropriation of fixed capital' by the producers (in antagonism with the enterprise, which is motivated by profit), I am in fact returning to a theme that had a great resonance in the past fifty years in the field of philosophy and politics. In German anthropology (with Plessner, Gehlen and Popitz), in French materialism (Simondon), and in materialist feminism (Haraway and Braidotti), the notion of hybridization between humans and machines has been amply developed. Here I would also refer to Guattari's theory of *agencements machiniques* [mechanical assemblages], which is more or less present in all his thinking and largely influences the philosophical design of *A Thousand Plateaus*. Probably the most important thing that has happened in these philosophical propositions is the fact that their positioning – which is homogeneously materialist despite the many different forms in which it presents itself – has revealed new characteristics, irreducible to any previous qualifications. Certainly, it has long been the case that materialism no longer appears in the epic guise in which the authors of the Enlightenment, the likes of d'Holbach and Helvetius, had elaborated it, and that has absorbed decisively dynamic aspects from twentieth-century physics. Now, in the theories I have mentioned, it is rather characterized by a 'humanist' [*'umanistica'*] imprint – which, far from renewing idealist apologies of the 'human being' [*dell' 'uomo'*], is defined by an interest in the body, in singularity, and in the density of this in thinking and operating. Today materialism looks like a theory of production, broadly balanced on cognitive aspects and on the effects of the cooperative hybridization of production itself. Is it the change in the mode of production, from the predominance of the material to the hegemony of the immaterial, that has generated these effects on philosophical thought? I am not fond of theories of mirroring,

so I don't think so – however, I am convinced of the association between the growth of the digital mode of production and this big change of and in the tradition of materialism. And here is an additional observation, which makes it possible to move towards an answer to the question raised initially: is the 'appropriation of fixed capital' a political metaphor? It certainly is, when we draw from this assumption a definition of power [*potenza*], for example, in political and possibly constituent terms, and when the appropriation of fixed capital becomes the analogical basis for the construction of an ethical or political subject, adapted to a materialist ontology of the present and to a communist teleology of the future, the to-come [*a-venire*].

3. But the development of the notion of 'appropriation of fixed capital' is not always metaphorical. Marx began to show how the mere placement of workers vis-à-vis (the command of) the means of production modified not only their productive capacity but also their figure, their nature, their ontology. The Marxian narrative of the transition from 'manufacturing' to 'big industry' is typical from this point of view. In manufacturing there is still a 'subjective' principle in division of labour – and this means that the worker appropriated the production process after the production process had been adapted to the worker (*Capital* vol. 1.2, pp. 457–8, 501–2),[2] whereas in big industry the division of labour is only 'objective', the subjective and artisanal use of the machine having been eliminated (pp. 588–9), and machinery turns against the human (pp. 535–7, 539, 547–8, 562–4). Furthermore, the machine reveals itself to be competitive with, antagonistic to, the worker (vol. 2.2, pp. 552–4, 558–9), or indeed reduces the worker to a working animal (vol. 3.1, p. 179–80). And yet one also finds in Marx a different starting point: he recognizes that the worker and the means of labour also configure themselves as a hybrid construction and that the conditions of the production process constitute in large part the workers' living conditions, their 'form of life' (pp. 176, 179–81). The very concept of productivity of labour implies a close and dynamic connection between variable capital and fixed capital (pp. 318–19, 368–70), and theoretical discoveries, adds Marx, are taken up in the production process through the experience of the worker (p. 199). Later on I shall conclude by discussing how, in *Capital*, Marx himself perceives the appropriation of fixed capital by the producer.

Now, I should stress that Marx's analysis in *Capital* is underpinned by the position argued in the *Grundrisse*, namely the theorization of general intellect* as the material and subject of the production process. This discovery made it possible to show the extent to which cognitive matter was central to production and how the concept of fixed capital itself was transformed by it. When Marx proclaims that fixed capital, which in *Capital* is normally understood as a complex of machines, has become the human person itself [*'l'uomo stesso', der Mensch selbst*], he is anticipating the development of capital in our time. Although fixed capital is the product of labour and nothing but labour appropriated by capital, although the accumulation of scientific activity and the productivity of what Marx calls 'social intellect' are incorporated in machines under the control of capital, and, finally, although capital appropriates all this for free – at some point in capitalist development living labour begins to exercise the power to reverse this relationship. Living labour begins to show its priority over capital and over the capitalist management† of social production, even if this management cannot necessarily be taken out of the process. In other words, when it becomes an increasingly wider social power, living labour operates as an increasingly independent activity, outside the disciplinary structures that capital commands – not only as labour power but also, more generally, as life activity. On the one hand, human activity in the past and its intelligence are accumulated and crystallized as fixed capital; but on the other hand, reversing the flow, living human beings are able to reabsorb capital into themselves and into their social life. Fixed capital is 'the human person' in both senses.

Here the appropriation of fixed capital is no longer a metaphor; it becomes a *dispositif* that the class struggle can take on and that imposes itself as a political programme. In this case capital is no longer a relationship that objectively includes the producer, imposing its dominion by force. Rather the capitalist relationship now contains an ultimate contradiction: that of a producer, of a class of producers, that has, partially or totally but anyway effectively, deprived this relationship of the means of production by imposing itself as a hegemonic subject. The analogy with the emergence of the third estate in the structures of the ancien régime is pursued by Marx in the historicization of the relation of capital and clearly shows itself in an explosive and revolutionary manner.

---

* 'General intellect' in English in the original (here and passim).
† 'Management' in English in the original (here and passim).

4. At this point we need to turn our attention to the new figures of labour, especially those created by the workers themselves, in social networks.* These are the workers whose productive capacities have been dramatically increased by their increasingly intense cooperation. Now, let's look at what happens here. In cooperation, work becomes more and more detached from capital – that is, it has a greater capacity to organize production itself, independently, and especially in relation to machines, while remaining subordinate to the mechanisms of extraction of labour by capital. Is this the same autonomy that we recognized in the forms of independent labour, in the early stages of capitalist production? Certainly not, I would say. The hypothesis is that now there is a measure of autonomy that not only involves the process of production but imposes itself in an ontological sense as well – that labour acquires an ontological consistency even when it is completely subordinated to capitalist command. How can we understand a situation in which productive enterprises, temporally continuous and spatially extended, and collective and cooperative inventions made by workers end up being fixed as value extracted from capital? This will be difficult, unless we shake off linear and deterministic methodologies and assume a method articulated through *dispositifs*. Thus it can be recognized that this is a situation in which the relationship between productive processes in the hands of workers and capitalist mechanisms of value creation and command get increasingly separated. Labour has reached such a level of dignity and power that it can in principle reject the form of valorization that is imposed on it and therefore, even under command, develop its own autonomy.

The increasing powers of labour can be recognized not only in the expansion and increasing autonomy of cooperation but also in the greater importance given to the social and cognitive powers of labour in the structures of production. The first element, an expanded cooperation, is certainly due to the increase of physical contact between digital workers in computerized society but, even more (as Paolo Virno has always urged us to think), to the formation of a 'mass intellectuality' animated by linguistic and cultural competences, by emotional abilities and by digital potentialities. As for the second element, it is no coincidence that these skills and this creativity of labour increase productivity. Let us consider, then, how the role of knowledge has changed in the history of the relationship between capital

---

* 'Social networks' in English in the original.

and labour. As we have already seen, in the manufacturing phase, the knowledge of artisanal workers was employed and absorbed into production as a separate, isolated, and thereby subordinate force within a hierarchical organizational structure. In the big industry phase, on the other hand, the workers were considered incapable of the knowledge necessary for production, which was therefore centralized into the hands of management. In the contemporary phase of general intellect, knowledge has a multitudinous form in the production process, even if, from the point of view of the bosses, it can be isolated, as was the artisans' knowledge in manufacturing. In reality, from the point of view of capital, the way in which labour organizes itself remains an enigma, even when this becomes the basis of production.

To take one example, a powerful figure of associated labour is hidden today under the functioning of algorithms. Alongside the incessant propaganda that affirms the necessity of the capitalist command and lectures on the unavoidable alternative to this system of power, we often hear praises for the role of the algorithm. But what is an algorithm? In the first place it is fixed capital: a machine born of social cooperative intelligence, a product of general intellect. Although the value of a productive activity is fixed in the social process of extracting surplus labour from capital, it must not be forgotten that the strength of living labour is the basis of this process. Without living labour there is no algorithm. However, the algorithms have numerous new features: this is a second point. Consider Google's PageRank, perhaps the best known and most profitable algorithm of all. Now, the rank* of a web page is determined by the number and quality of links, and high quality means a link to a page that has a high rank itself. PageRank is therefore a mechanism for incorporating the judgement and value granted by users to Internet objects. According to Matteo Pasquinelli, each link is a concentrate of intelligence. Nevertheless, the relevant difference of algorithms such as those of Google's PageRank is that, while industrial machines crystallize past intelligence in a relatively fixed and static form, those algorithms continuously add social intelligence to the results of the past, in order to create an open and expansive dynamic. It looks as if the algorithmic machine itself were intelligent – but that is not the case; rather it is open to the continuous modifications of human intelligence. When we say 'intelligent machines', we must understand by it machines

---

* All the occurrences of 'rank', 'link' and 'web page' are in English in the original.

that are continuously capable of absorbing intelligence. A second distinctive sign is that the process of extractive value established by these algorithms is itself incrementally opened and is socialized so as to exclude the boundaries between work and life. Google users know this well . . . Finally, another difference between the productive processes studied by Marx and this kind of value production consists in the fact that cooperation today is no longer imposed by the bosses but is generated in the relationship between producers. Today we really can speak of a reappropriation of fixed capital by workers and of an integration of intelligent machines under autonomous social control – identifying it, for example, in a process of constructing algorithms that favour the self-enhancement of social cooperation and of the reproduction of life.

One could add that, even when cybernetic and digital tools are used in the service of capitalist enhancement, even when social intelligence is put to work and called upon to produce obedient subjectivities, fixed capital is integrated into the bodies and brains of workers and becomes their second nature. Ever since industrial civilization was born, workers have had a more intimate insider's knowledge of machines and machine systems than the capitalists and their managers could possibly gain. Today, these processes of workers' appropriation of knowledge can become decisive They are not realized simply in production processes, but are intensified and concretized through productive cooperation in the vital processes of circulation and socialization. Operators can appropriate fixed capital while they work, and they can develop this appropriation in their social, cooperative and biopolitical relationships with other workers. All this brings about a new productive nature, in other words a new 'form of life' that forms the basis of the new 'mode of production'.

5.   To go even deeper into the subject and to remove the apparent utopianism that, even without damaging my argument, sometimes seems to confuse it, let us consider how some scholars of cognitive capitalism organize the hypothesis of the appropriation of fixed capital. I shall be very brief and refer to Harvey, who has studied this appropriation through the analysis of spaces of settlement and of metropolises traversed by bodies put to work – translocations of the variable capital that have radical effects on the conditions and practices of subjected bodies still capable of autonomous movements and of autonomy in the organization of work. However, his analysis is rather external. Much more incisive is the position that Gorz suggested in his time, reversing the complex interplay of exploitation and

alienation and emphasizing that the intellectual powers of production are formed in the social body. Liberation from social alienation relaunches the ability to act subjectively and intellectually in production. As we proceed along this line, we are not surprised to discover, with Vercellone, that, in the global stock of capital today, the kind of capital we call 'intangible' – R&D, and also education and health – exceeds material capital and has become the determining element of economic growth. Fixed capital appears now in bodies, engraved in them and at the same time subordinated to them – all the more as we consider activities such as research or software, where work does not crystallize in a material product separate from the worker but remains incorporated in the brain, indissociable from physical persons.[3] Laurent Baronian makes a crucial point when, returning to capital and the analysis of the relations of production, he generalizes the power of bodies and minds by taking their association as the qualifying element of fixed capital. Here fixed capital is social cooperation. Here the boundaries of the relationship between living labour and dead labour (or between variable capital and fixed capital) are definitively confused.

Indeed, as Marx concludes in *Capital* in this regard, if, from the point of view of the capitalist, constant capital is identical with variable capital under the heading of circulating capital (*Capital* vol. 3.1, pp. 123–4, 165–9, 252–3, 374–5) and the only difference essential to the capitalist is that between fixed capital and circulating capital (pp. 167–9, 252–3), it follows that, from the point of view of the producer, constant capital is identical with circulating capital under the heading of fixed capital and the only essential difference is that between variable capital and fixed capital: it is on fixed capital that variable capital now focuses all its interest in reappropriation.

The emancipatory conditions of the cooperation of living labour therefore invest and increasingly occupy the spaces and functions of fixed capital.

More on this point – from Vercellone and Marazzi: what is called immaterial or intellectual capital is in reality essentially incorporated in human beings, and therefore fundamentally corresponds to the intellectual and creative faculties of labour power. We are faced with an upheaval of the very concepts of constant capital and organic composition of capital inherited from industrial capitalism. In the ratio between fixed capital (C) and variable capital (V), which defines mathematically the social organic composition of capital, it is in fact labour power (V) that appears as the principal fixed capital and – to adopt Christian Marazzi's expression – as the 'body machine' of 'labour power'. This is because, as Marazzi points out, 'in addition to containing the faculty of labour, it also acts as a container of the typical functions of fixed capital and of the means of production qua sedimentation of codified knowledge, historically acquired knowledges, productive grammars, experiences – in short, past labour'.[4]

6.   Machinic subjectivities: this, for example, is how we could qualify young people who enter the digital world spontaneously. We conceive of *the machinic* by contrast not only with the mechanical but also with the notion of a separate technological reality, one that is even opposed to human society. Félix Guattari explains that, whereas traditionally the problem of machines has been seen as secondary to the issue of *technē* and technology, we must rather recognize that the problem of machines is primary and that of technology comes second. According to him, we can see the social nature of the machine; the concept of technological machine must be expanded to that of *agencements machiniques* from the moment when the machine opens up to a machinic environment and maintains all sorts of relationships with its social constituents and individual subjectivities. Therefore the machinic never refers to an isolated individual machine but always to an assemblage. To understand this, we begin to think of mechanical systems, in other words of machines connected to and integrated with other machines. We then add human subjectivities; we imagine humans integrated into machinic relationships and machines integrated into human bodies and into human society. Finally, together with Deleuze, Guattari conceives of machinic assemblages as progressive, as incorporating all kinds of human elements and human and non-human singularities. The concept of the machinic in Deleuze and Guattari and – later, in a different form – the concept of production in Foucault capture the need to develop subjectivities of knowledge and action outside spiritualist identities and to demonstrate how they emerge from productive activities that are materially connected.

   In economic terms, the machinic appears clearly in the subjectivities that emerge when fixed capital is reappropriated by labour power, that is, when the material and immaterial machines and the knowledges that crystallize social production from the past are reintegrated into the social subjectivities that cooperate and produce in the present. Machinic assemblages are thus partly grasped in the notion of anthropogenic production. Some of the most intelligent Marxist economists, such as Robert Boyer and Christian Marazzi, characterize the novelty of contemporary economic production – and the transition from Fordism to post-Fordism – by focusing on '*la production de l'homme par l'homme*', 'the production of human by human', in contrast with the traditional notion of the production of commodities by means of commodities. Subjectivity production and life forms become increasingly central to capitalist valorization, and this logic leads directly to the notions of cognitive and biopolitical production. The machinic extends this anthropogenetic model further in order to incorporate various non-human singularities in the ensembles that it produces and that are produced. More to the point, when we say that fixed capital is reappropriated by working subjects, we do not simply say that it becomes their possession but rather that it is integrated into machinic assemblages, which constitute subjectivity.

The machinic is always an assembly, a dynamic composition of human and other beings, but the power of these new machinic subjectivities is only virtual, until it comes to be actualized and articulated in social cooperation and in the common. If the reappropriation of the fixed capital really took place individually, by transferring private property from one individual to another, it would be just an act of robbing Peter to pay Paul and would have no real meaning. When, on the other hand, the wealth and productive power of fixed capital is socially appropriated, in other words when it is shifted from private property to the common, then the power [*potere*] of machinic subjectivities and their cooperative networks can be fully actualized. The machinic dynamics of assembly, the productive forms of cooperation and the ontological basis of the common become inextricably intertwined.

When we look at today's young people, absorbed as they are in the common and moulded into forms of cooperation by their machinic undertakings, we need to understand that their true existence is resistance. Whether they are aware of it or not, they produce resistance. Capital is forced to come to terms with this harsh truth. It can consolidate economically the development of that common that is the product of subjectivities – subjectivities from which it extracts value; but the common is built only through those forms of resistance and those processes that reappropriate fixed capital. The contradiction becomes increasingly clear. Capital tells the productive subjectivities 'exploit yourself', and they reply: 'we wish to valorize ourselves; we wish to govern the common that we produce'. No obstacle to this process – not even the suspicion of virtual obstacles – can prevent the confrontation from approaching. If capital can expropriate value only from the cooperation of subjectivities, and if these resist exploitation, then capital must raise the level of command and implement operations of extracting value from the common that are increasingly arbitrary and violent. It is to these transitions that the notion of reappropriation of fixed capital leads us.

'The Platforms of Capitalism' seminar, Macao, Milan,
3–4 March 2017

7

General Intellect and the Social Individual in Marx's *Grundrisse**

1

I can hardly begin to tell you how happy I am to be at the Volksbühne, to present and discuss the German translation of my *Marx oltre Marx* [*Marx beyond Marx*] for the prestigious Berlin publishing house Dietz Verlag. This is a book that was written at the end of the long decade of 1968–79, during which I was deeply engaged with class struggles in Italy and in Europe, and it arose out of lectures that I was giving in Paris in 1978, at the École Normale Supérieure, at the invitation of Louis Althusser.

The book was born out of a rereading of the *Grundrisse*, as a way of locating Marx in the struggles of those years, and in the hope of an upcoming working-class revolution. It was part and parcel of those struggles and fulfilled what it set out to achieve, reaffirming Marx as a source of revolutionary subjectivation. In this instance, as they say, *habent sua fata libella* [books have their own destiny].

---

* Paper first published in 2019 in EuroNomade under the title 'General intellect e individuo sociale nei grundrisse marxiani': visit http://www.euronomade. info/?p=12059. The paper was prepared for a public meeting at the Volksbühne, Berlin, 29 April 2019, which could not be held because the author was indisposed. Sections 6–7 contain material that overlaps with large sections of Chapter 6 in this volume.

2

Returning to this book today (and, with it, to this Marx), what does it tell us? Or, if we want to put it in terms less related to the book and to the events that inspired it, what can the *Grundrisse* tell us in and of the situation of capitalism today?

To answer, we need first to identify the core, fundamental characteristics of capitalism in the twenty-first century.

I shall acknowledge the dominant role of finance capital to begin with and, after that, the extractive, logistical and biopolitical dimensions of capitalist accumulation today; and, third, I shall try to define the new spaces of anticapitalist subjectivation and class struggle today.

2.1

On the first point, it is clear that, when we take on board the theory of finance capital laid out in volume 3 of *Capital* and in the 'Chapter on Money' in the *Grundrisse*, it opens to a fundamental aspect of today's capitalism. This is a place where the becoming autonomous of the 'general equivalent' and its openness to the world market – which could be the presupposition and the result of everything – allow us to grasp the characteristics of today's finance capital and to go well beyond the fictitious, the speculative and the parasitic – categories in critical theory that neutralize its function and its hegemonic position. Today finance capital is rather the central point of capitalist command: money as a 'general equivalent' not only represents the function of *measuring and regulating* global production; it is also the central productive matrix, the engine of accumulation. It is through finance capital that a new division of labour has been established at the global level, and it is here that the internal struggles between the components of global collective capital have been opened and closed, and now open again. These struggles aim to determine decisive relations of force.

2.2

The second point concerns the concept's opening to the *biopolitical*. As we know, in our present times capital has reached the point of real subsumption, of complete absorption of society. This is a major historical transition, which was complete by the end of the twentieth century. In this context, exploitation changes. Now it is exerted over life itself, and consists in the *extraction* of value from nature and from social cooperation. This takes place through production and circulation (the one inside the other), through machines that invest and connect the territories of and within subsumption; and the operating machine for the communication and distribution of what is extracted from cooperation is *logistics*. It is within this complex situation that the intuition of something 'beyond' industrial production – an intuition initially built up in Marx's 'Fragment on Machines' – comes to be applied to the Marxian analysis of capitalist development. In fact the 'Fragment' makes us understand the current mode of production and the role that digital machines [*le macchine numeriche*] have played and continue to play in the postindustrial era, as a means of exploitation of cognitive labour.

In 1978, when we already embarked on this interpretation of the 'Fragment', we were really on our own. This interpretation was then taken up by many other authors, so that today, when we speak of real subsumption, we can say that it invests the whole of society and that exploitation is essentially exercised in the form of *extraction* from cooperative social labour and through the capture of the excess of surplus value that this cooperation creates. A few passages from the *Grundrisse* suffice to give the measure of the correctness of our intuition, and also of the extraordinary transformations we have witnessed:

> As the basis on which large industry rests, the appropriation of alien labour time ceases, with its development, to make up or to create wealth, so does direct labour as such cease to be the basis of production, since, in one respect, it is transformed more into a supervisory and regulatory activity; but then also because the product ceases to be the product of isolated direct labour, and the *combination* of social activity appears, rather, as the producer. (*Grundrisse*, p. 709)[1]

And from this derive extraordinary consequences, to which I shall return. ('For real wealth is the developed productive power of all individuals. The measure of wealth is then not any longer, in any way, labour time, but rather disposable time', p. 708).

2.3

The third point, which is particularly developed in the *Grundrisse* and allows us to arrive at a reading of capitalism today, relates to the statement that the true non-capital is labour. Now, this statement breaks with every conception that might seek to tie into a necessary common nexus the development of the productive forces of human labour and the development of capital. No, this relationship is a relation of force that brings about various compositions of that division (between 'use value' and 'exchange value' of labour power) which is at the root of the concept of capital. As Tronti says, 'when we are talking about the working class within the system of capital, the same productive force really can be counted twice: one time as a force that produces capital and another time as a force that refuses to produce it; one time within capital, another time against capital'.[2] Stabilizing and dominating this nexus has represented the historical victory of the collective capitalist. But at the origins there is a split, a duality; there is a balance of forces and a rupture that will never be definitively closed. And it is from this rupture, from the power that is expressed in living labour, that the development of capital was born. This is what the *Grundrisse* teaches us. There would be no surplus value if there were no surplus labour, but surplus labour would not produce capital if it were only surplus value: it is instead, at the origins, 'non-capital', it is creative excedence.

The Hegelian formula is useful at this point: the negative, that which is vital, anticipates and qualifies what it produces. But here the Hegelian metaphor, so dear to the 'theorists of recognition' of the Frankfurt School, breaks down – because the splitting is neither healed nor overcome. What explains surplus value as a symbol of exploitation is the fact that exchange is a theft and that the equivalent is a swindle. According to Vygotsky, this concept of surplus value was discovered by Marx in the *Grundrisse*, and the concept of relative surplus value was fixed by Marx there as a value proportional to the living labour consumed in the process of capitalist production. These concepts, always based on the refrain 'the real non-capital is labour', explain the process of propagation of the productive force of capital. It arises, indeed, from relative surplus value, but this can lead to a situation in which surplus value no longer corresponds simply to an increase in surplus labour by way of *lengthening* of the working day, but rather to an increase by way of *reducing* the necessary labour; it can lead to a positive transvaluation of the power [*potenza*] of living labour, an increase in its productive capacity, paradoxically, as 'non-capital'. Here we are at the root of the antagonism brought about by living labour: it calls into play an unobjectified labour power. This is also the historical transition that the *Grundrisse* anticipates and explains: from 'formal subsumption' to 'real subsumption' – and it is only here that *life* comes to be wholly included in capitalist development. But this is where the class struggle explodes, in the face of the primary contradiction of the capital relationship: that of being a relationship of antagonism.

3

So let me summarize before proceeding further with the analysis. The phenomenology of real subsumption, of cooperation and of the excedence of living labour, and of the global monetary regime offers us a picture of capital as *extraction*, *logistics* and *financialization*: this is the form of domination we live in. These are the fundamental characteristics of capital accumulation today. And yet not even in this absolute form is capital a leviathan. It is a class *relationship*, a dual figure. In the *Grundrisse*, fixed in its absolute power, capital is flanked by the workers' cooperation, which presents itself in the form of a *social individual*.

3.1

Who and what is the social individual? Let us first see what the worker has become today. This is someone who operates in an immaterial network, where employers increase productivity at the same time as they extract surplus value from it. On the other hand, these workers, located as they are in an increasingly intense cooperation of labour, develop a growing productive capacity and affirm their cooperative productivity as the driving force of the production system, in an increasingly evident manner.

Let me explain: within cooperation, labour becomes more and more 'abstract', in other words, more and more expressive of the value of production and more and more central to the ability to organize production. At the same time, however, this consolidated ensemble of abstract labour is more and more heavily subjected to operations of extraction of the value produced. In other words, on the one hand workers are increasingly placed in the condition of creating cooperation, and hence productivity, and on the other they suffer increasingly the effects of capital's extraction of the value produced; in their relationship with machinery, workers develop the aspect of cooperation with increasing autonomy, but in doing so they also organize the extraction of their own productive energy.

So then, can we still speak, in a situation of real subsumption, of a *relative* autonomy of the worker, in the sense in which we were able to do it earlier, in the phase of formal subsumption of labour under capital? Then the artisan, the independent worker, found a productive position within the industrial system, and was thus valued in this difference and interiority. This doesn't hold any longer, because the degree of autonomy of postindustrial workers doesn't rely now simply on their having a different position in the production cycle; it depends on their participation in the cooperative processes of production. But this position has a paradoxically autonomous element, even though it is subjected to capitalist command. Here a situation is created in which a temporally continuous and spatially extended autonomous productive initiative and a collective and cooperating inventivity are subordinated to the extraction of value by capital. This is a major change, which we experience when the labour process (in the hands of the workers) and the capitalist process of value creation, which have always been separated in form, begin to be separated in reality too, the former being relegated to the autonomy of living labour, the latter to pure command. This means that labour has reached a level of dignity and strength that is in contradiction with the form of valorization imposed on it.

For example, when people talk of the efficacy 'without alternatives' of the power of capital that the single thought [*pensiero unico*] of bosses and social democrats produces ('there is no alternative'),* we hear more and more praises sung to the rule of the 'algorithm'. But what is this algorithm, to which is attributed the mastering of the digital processes of capitalist valorization today? It is nothing but a 'machine' born from the cooperation of workers, from logistic intellectuality, and that the bosses impose on this cooperation – more precisely, on this mass intellectuality. The algorithm is the bosses' machine over mass intellectuality. The big difference between the labour processes studied by Marx and today's labour processes is that today cooperation has stopped being imposed by the bosses but is produced from within the cooperation of the workforce; the production process and the machines are not brought from outside by the employer but are internalized, appropriated by the workers. We can speak properly of an 'appropriation of fixed capital' by workers, and with this we would indicate a process of construction of the cognitive algorithm, disposed to the valorization of labour in all its articulations, capable of producing languages of which it will become

---

* 'There is no alternative' in English in the original.

dominus [the master]. These languages were therefore created by workers, who possess both their key and their cooperative engine.

(Let it be clear that I don't consider here labour cooperation, its relative autonomy, as something that can be *immediately* transformed into a subject, into a collective individual, and even less as something that can be thought of as a fully formed subject. The transition from technical composition to political composition is always discontinuous, unpredictable, and determined only by history. But this does not mean that the 'social individual' is not being formed, is not there. Here it seems to me fundamental to grasp that labour power attains an ever higher dignity under capitalist development. It is fundamental to repropose this idea in an age of metaphysical catastrophisms and political maledictions that assail labour power and increasingly diminish its potency [*potenza*] and dignity, at the same time as individualizing it and consigning it to a destiny of subordination.)

3.2

If this is the case, it is only by pursuing the progressive abstraction of labour processes that capitalist command succeeds in exercising itself. It is no coincidence that we no longer talk about simple exploitation, tied to the industrial dimensions of labour organization, but of an extractive exploitation of social cooperation. In this type of value creation, the organization of labour is primarily an *agencement* [arrangement] (interconnection, exercise, *dispositif* . . .) of the production of subjectivity – where by 'production of subjectivity' I mean on the one hand production through 'subjectivation' (in other words, the activation of the singular qualities and knowledges of worker-subjects) and, on the other hand, the continuous attempt to reduce the latter, their singularity, to being 'subjects' under command. Subjectivation means that, within the new form of work organization (that is, in 'real subsumption' and through the biopolitical agency [*operare*] of the producer), *the worker is subjectivated* to the utmost – both because cooperation is a social fact, which therefore requires the composition of a plurality in an operative ensemble, and because labour has become more and more immaterial; and by 'immaterial' I mean that it is cognitive, affective, tertiary, and so on (and is thus the expression of a creative singularity whose productive power cannot simply be considered a statistical variant of the law of value). Taking this process to its limit, Marx will say that fixed capital is now the human person itself: a collective individual that recomposes the production process within its own component parts.

In this figure are presented the *different figures* of living labour in its *postindustrial structuring*. And we should bear in mind that, when capital identified that new rich context in which living labour expresses itself and placed it under its command, it acted in two ways. On the one hand, it articulated its command in the living production of languages; on the other, it operated through a functionalization, to capitalist command, of the worker's needs and desires. Capital (in neoliberalism) would like the power of productive *subjectivation* to be recognized as the subject of the relationship of capital. It would want voluntary servitude. I believe that, seen from a class point of view, this contradictory experience constitutes a limit for capitalist value creation.

3.3

Given all this, I can now restate the question more clearly: who or what is the social individual today?

To answer this question, one can follow two paths, which correspond to the double position that the social individual has in the relationship of domination defined by capital today. The first is the path that allows us to consider the social individual from the *objective* point of view, as a machine of capital. The second will present the social individual from the subjective point of view, in other words as subjectivity, as subjectivation capable of liberation.

So this brings me back to the capital–labour relation, the relationship between fixed capital and variable capital – but situates it in a period in which the *collective*, cooperative character of the production process and its relative *autonomy* can no longer be denied. Variable capital has, then, a collective figure, is built in cooperation, and is defined in cognitive terms. The point of contradiction, determined by the antagonistic relationship of capital, is thus established on the terrain of the cognitive. Economists would call it the terrain of 'knowledge economy'. Two research hypotheses are given on it. The first is, so to speak, *external*: knowledge [*conoscenza*], incorporated in labour and mobilized by it, is described within the technical and social division of labour and of the institutional mechanisms that bring about a general level of *Bildung* (training, education) for the entire working class. The second option is instead *internal*, so to speak: knowledge is incorporated by capital and somehow presents itself as a form of fixed capital. But its appearance in this guise, as fixed capital, is highly ambiguous. Actually collective labour power is on the one hand absorbed in the technology and logistics of the bosses (thus it is variable capital), but on the other hand has the ability to express itself in autonomous forms, as we have seen, and therefore to appropriate fixed capital.

3.3.1 It is important in the first place to highlight the *external* relationship. It is especially here that the social conditions of productive cooperation and the collective productions of the welfare state* are determined. Here are developed those modes of the 'production of the human for the human' [*'produzione dell'uomo per l'uomo'*] that constitute the polarity of labour power in its relationship with capital and that shape and defend the relative autonomy of variable capital (as well as the autonomy of living labour). In this context, the knowledge economy that arises from the encounter of collective intelligence with the development of welfare institutions, and finally with the technical institutions of the digital revolution (if addressed from a critical point of view), exhibits a vigorous life force. And this dynamic comes directly into contradiction with the logic of cognitive capitalism – a logic based on the commodification, ownership and corporatization of knowledge. This line of *external* relationship between capital and cognitive labour is really fundamental. To demonstrate its importance, one has to identify the forms in which the functioning of welfare constitutes an enormous space of production of knowledge and a real counterpower. Carlo Vercellone has written a lot about these figures.

3.3.2 This emphasis serves to flag the other line, the one I called *internal*, and thus to make one analyse and assume as a protagonist figure, apart from the effects of the clash between constant capital and variable capital on the social terrain, the *appropriation of fixed capital* by workers, in other words by living labour.

This specification assumes growing importance insofar as the capitalist mode of production *intersects* living labour in its cognitive form. It intersects it in the sense that it exploits it, extracts value from it, and tries to appropriate it, but at the same time it clashes with it, with its relative autonomy. 'The roar of battle is heard', said someone who studied this intersection. If living cognitive labour, extended and diffused on the biopolitical terrain, then becomes the force that clashes with capitalist accumulation (what I have called the *external* scenario), it is also true that constant capital becomes flexible in this

---

* 'Welfare state' in English in the original.

clash, diffuses itself more and more on the social terrain of production, and clashes with the individual performances of the productive
subjects, with the self-valorization of living labour. On this terrain,
where constant capital seems to make itself flexible in confrontation
with living labour and where the productive power of capital seems to
yield to the power of living labour (variable capital), the *internal* path
of the appropriation of fixed capital by living labour becomes increasingly central and substantial.

4

Now we come to the central argument for seeing how the theoretical
effects of the doctrine of the general intellect are realized. In fact it is
possible to identify here, starting from the continuity of the process
of subsumption from formal to real, a third form of subsumption
of society in capital – namely subsumption under general intellect.
The formation of general intellect corresponds, as we know, to the
structural crisis of industrial capitalism, as brought about by workers'
struggles (without underestimating the already important qualitative preponderance of knowledge in the living labour incorporated
into fixed capital). The 'regulation school' had already advanced the
hypothesis of a *third phase* of subsumption, associated with the identification of general intellect – as Vercellone reminds us again.

4.1

How does this third subsumption look? Permit me first to express a
concern. We must not work with this subsumption as if there were
a *teleological* chain of events, as if we were dealing with a consecutive
transition from one form of subsumption to another. The development between stages of subsumption is not teleological; history
is not a linear process, it proceeds rather through hybridizations
and overlappings, articulations and alternatives between modes of
accumulation. The same is true of the figures of subsumption: they
appear in a discontinuous and jagged manner, hybrid and overlap-
ping. What we can say is that this process is *tendential*. What does
'tendential' mean here? A tendency does not imply a deterministic
direction, a Darwinian movement; it certainly means evolution, but
this evolution takes place in the interplay between tendency and countertendency (as *Capital* teaches us in several places). Consequently,
the organic composition of capital itself is always different, registering

the differential impact of the various figures of subsumption, social movements and workers' struggles, and it can therefore be seen as a composition discontinuously defined by relations of force between classes. *So, if there is tendency, there is also countertendency*: in the case we are studying, both the appropriation of fixed capital by workers and the consideration of welfare as a space for identifying an autonomy of variable capital lower the organic composition of capital. And it is this breach that allows us to grasp the birth of the *social individual* in the context of subsumption under general intellect.

4.2

So let us listen to what Marx had to say on this subject, to see more accurately how the social individual appears in the subsumption of general intellect. When one arrives at the highest moment of real subsumption, Marx writes, 'so does it appear in the further develoment of capital, that it presupposes a certain given historical development of the productive forces on one side – science too [is] among these productive forces – and on the other, drives and forces them further onwards' (*Grundrisse*, p. 699). Immediate labour thus disappears as a 'determinate principle' of production, because it is reduced to a 'smaller' and 'subordinate moment, compared to general scientific labour, technological application of natural sciences on one side, and to the general productive force arising from social combination in total production on the other side – a combination which appears as a natural fruit of social labour (although it a historical product)' (p. 700). So here we have it: general intellect as a force of subsumption at the centre of capital development.

> But to the degree that large industry develops, the creation of real wealth comes to depend less on labour time and on the amount of labour employed than on the power of the agencies set in motion during labour time, whose 'powerful effectiveness' is itself in turn out of all proportion to the direct labour time spent on their production, but depends rather on the general state of science, and on the progress of technology, or the application of this science to production. (*Grundrisse*, pp. 704–5)

4.3

But here is the breach: within and against general intellect there emerges the social individual, the name that the working class has assumed in subsumption under general intellect. The worker steps to the side of the production process instead of being its chief actor. In this transformation, it is neither the direct human labour he himself performs, nor the time during which he works, but rather the appropriation of his own general productive power, his understanding of nature and his mastery over it by virtue of his presence as a social body – it is, in a word, the development of the social individual which appears as the great foundation-stone of production and of wealth. (*Grundrisse*, p. 705)

Finally,

Nature builds no machines, no locomotives, railways, electric tele-graphs, self-acting mules etc. These are products of human industry; natural material transformed into organs of the human will over nature, or of human participation in nature. They are *organs of the human brain, created by the human hand*; the power of knowledge, objectified. The development of fixed capital indicates to what degree general social knowledge has become a *direct force of production*, and to what degree, hence, the conditions of the process of social life itself have come under the control of the general intellect and been transformed in accordance with it. To what degree the powers of social production have been pro-duced, not only in the form of knowledge, but also as immediate organs of social practice, of the real life process. (*Grundrisse*, p. 706)

5

We are now in a position to address directly the subjectivation of the social individual in general intellect, within subsumption. We know that this social individual embodies (gives flesh to) the abstraction of labour. We also know that in this way the abstraction of labour becomes a common power, because it is formed in the coopera-tion of the processes of production – a cooperation that has become more and more *extensive* and *intense* in the productive development of capital, to be fully realized in general intellect, in a third-degree subsumption. More and more *extensive* because, as we have seen, the capitalists' response to the struggles of the 1960s and 1970s was to escape from the factory – or, if they kept the factories, to empty them of workers. But, while fleeing the factory meant investing the whole of society with productive services and putting it to work towards the production of goods, for workers this meant building new forms of cooperation at the social level – always *subordinated to*, but often *independent from*, the direct command of capital. Spatial mobility and temporal flexibility were the forms in which the worker's *relative independence* in the new cooperation could be seen for a while. Capital then forced it into the *precarization* of the waged worker; but this creates a continuous instability and imbalances that are difficult to resolve.

And also increasingly *intense* because the second capitalist response to the great cycle of mass worker struggles consisted in the massive introduction of plant automation and the digitalization or computerization of labour, in addition to the spatial and social extension of labour processes. The subsumption of the spaces of social cooperation was thus accompanied by the subsumption, under general intellect, of new intellectual and linguistic energies of a new and better educated workforce. If the algorithm is a machine that runs to the places where it finds strikes, as old Marx might have said – in other words, to the places where there is resistance and rupture, and therefore restructuring, of the valorization process – it is a machine produced today by that same autonomous force, which is expressed by the new quality of living labour.

The general productivity of labour thus took a great leap forward. But above all the social cooperation of the productive subjects intensified, since cognitive labour lives on linguistic cooperation, on the knowledge that constitutes it, and on the singular innovation it produces. This is how *the independence of living labour* grows in the face of the dead labour that seeks to organize it. This is how *the common* of cooperation imposes itself.

5.1

This radical change in living labour produces the current difficulties of capital in the control of labour power and in the management of development. The Marxian social individual is not only a virtuality, it is also a mode, a given of the class struggle. It is that relative independence of living, social and cognitive labour, that cooperative common, which capital can no longer subordinate except through management *from above*. Once again, the old adage of *operaismo* [workerism] asserts itself: first the struggle, then the transformation, the capitalist restructuring. In fact the direct exploitation of individual labour – a characteristic of old management techniques – comes to be replaced by the *extraction* of social value by *finance*, through an increasingly rigid *governance* of social labour processes.

Let me turn at this point to underlining the characteristics of capitalism today: these are the definitions from which we started – but now let us consider them in the clash between the power of general intellect and the onset of the social individual. Then I should go on to review the traditional distinction between 'real' production and the monetary management of production. This distinction is impossible to maintain from a point of view internal to economic processes in general. In this framework, today capitalism is actually based on *rent*. The big industrialists, rather than reinvesting profit, recycle it through the mechanisms of rent. In the circuit of value creation, the lifeblood of capital is called today 'rent' and fulfils an essential function in the maintenance of the capitalist system. By this I mean the maintenance of social hierarchies and the unity of the command of capital. Money [*il denaro*] also becomes the only measure of social production. It is the form, the blood, the circulation and the reproduction in which the socially constructed value extracted from the entire economic system is consolidated. This is where the total subordination of society to capital takes place. Labour power, and hence the activity of society, is subsumed under this money, which is measure and at the same time control and command. The political class itself is entirely within this process, and the forms of politics dance to this tune.

5.2

The crisis of 2007, which seems never to end, can be interpreted on these assumptions. The crisis arises from the need to maintain order by multiplying currency [*moneta*] (the subprimes, and the whole scary mechanism that followed, functioned to help a banking system that was achieving world domination to pay for the social reproduction of a rebellious labour force). We therefore have to get our hands on *this thing*, if we want to destroy its capacity for resistance. There can be no quibble on this point. On the contrary, against every conception that assigns the reasons for the crisis to the separation between finance and 'real' production, I insist that financialization is not an unproductive and parasitic diversion of increasing shares of surplus value and collective saving. It is not a diversion; it is the new form taken by capital accumulation within the new processes of social and cognitive production of value. The financial crisis that we have seen developing must therefore be interpreted as a response to the blocking of capital accumulation produced by living labour on the global terrain – and as an implosive outcome, consequent on it, of the failure of capital accumulation, of difficulties in the processes of sorting out new forms of accumulation.

5.3

Let me return to the collective individual of the *Grundrisse*. It seems a rhetorical, strong, elegant, evocative turn of phrase, when Marx affirms, in this context, that fixed capital has become the human person itself. In reality, with this he anticipates the development of capital in our time. Although fixed capital is the product of labour and nothing but labour appropriated by capital, although the accumulation of scientific activity and the productivity of the social intellect are incorporated in machines under the control of capital, and, finally, although capital appropriates all this gratis – as I have already mentioned: as a *nature of sociality* [*come una natura della socialità*], of cooperation, and therefore for free – precisely this transformation allows us to grasp living labour as a power capable of subverting the capital relationship. Social individuals begin to show here their priority with respect to capital and the capitalist management of social production. In other words, when living labour becomes an ever-widening social power and appears as nature, when it operates as an activity increasingly independent of the disciplinary structures that capital commands, it stops showing only as labour power but presents itself in a more general way, as a *vital activity*. On the one hand, human activity and its past intelligence are accumulated and crystallized as fixed capital, but on the other, reversing the flow, living human beings are able to reabsorb capital into themselves and into their social life. Fixed capital is 'the human person' in both senses.

Here the appropriation of fixed capital is no longer a metaphor; it becomes a *dispositif* that the class struggle can assume and that imposes itself as a political programme. In this case capital is no longer just a relationship that includes the producer by forcefully imposing its dominion, but a capitalist relationship that now contains a further contradiction: that of a producer, a class of producers, social individuals who have, partially or totally but anyway effectively, emptied it of its power, revealing themselves to be hegemonic subjects. The analogy with the emergence of the third estate from within the structures of the *ancien régime*, as narrated by Marx in his history of class struggle, seems appropriate here – and also the explosive, revolutionary manner in which it is narrated. In short, class struggle for power is reborn here.

6

At this point we need to bring the new figures of labour into focus, especially those that, in digital labour, are created by the workers themselves. These are the workers whose productive capacities have been heightened by their increasingly intense cooperation. They are the leading element of the social individual. Now, let us look at what happens here. Cooperative labour has a great capacity for organizing production on its own, independently, and especially in relation to machines, while remaining subordinate to capital's mechanisms for extracting value. Is this the same autonomy that we recognized in the forms of self-employment, in the early stages of capitalist production? As I have already said, certainly not. The hypothesis is that now there is a degree of autonomy that not only concerns the process of production but imposes itself ontologically – that labour acquires an ontological consistency even when it is completely subordinated to capitalist command. This is what I mean by the *social individual*. Here we can recognize a situation in which productive processes in the hands of workers and capitalist mechanisms of valorization and command get increasingly separated. Labour has reached such a level of dignity and power that it can in principle reject the form of valorization that is imposed on it and therefore, even under command, develop its own autonomy.

6.1

Other than in the expansion and heightened autonomy of cooperation, the growing powers of the social individual can be recognized in the social and cognitive powers of labour within the structures of production. In the first place, expansive cooperation is certainly due to the increase in physical contact between digital workers in computerized society, but, as Paolo Virno urges us to consider, even more to the formation of a 'mass intellectuality' animated by linguistic and cultural skills, by emotional abilities and digital powers. These skills and this creativity of labour increase productivity the more singular they are – in other words, the more independent they are in their capacity for invention. Let us reflect, then, on how the role of knowledge has changed in the history of the relationship between capital and labour. As we have already seen, in the manufacturing phase, the knowledge of the artisan was employed and absorbed in production as a separate, isolated, and therefore subordinate force within a hierarchical organizational structure. In the big industry phase, on the other hand, the workers were considered incapable of the knowledge necessary for production, which was therefore centralized in management. In the contemporary phase of general intellect, knowledge has a multitudinous form in the production process, even if, from the point of view of the bosses, it must be isolated, as was the artisan knowledge in manufacturing. In reality, from the point of view of capital, the way in which labour organizes itself remains an enigma, even when this becomes the basis of production.

6.2

To enter into the matter more deeply and to remove the appearance of utopianism that might weaken my argument, let us consider how some scholars of cognitive capitalism have described the emergence of the social individual. I shall be very brief and refer to David Harvey, who studies this emergence through an analysis of spaces of settlement and the crossing of metropolises traversed by bodies put to work – repositionings of variable capital that have radical negative effects on the conditions and practices of the subjected bodies and that discover in them, nevertheless, capacities for autonomous movements and autonomy in the organization of labour. But this analysis is rather external. Much more incisive was the one that André Gorz suggested at the time, reversing the complex interplay of exploitation and alienation and highlighting how the intellectual potentialities of production are formed in the body of society. It is the liberation from social alienation that relaunches the capacity to act subjectively and intellectually in production. As one proceeds along this line, one is not surprised to discover, with Carlo Vercellone, that, in the global stock of capital today, the kind of capital we call 'intangible' – R&D, and also education and health – exceeds material capital and has become the determining element of economic growth. Fixed capital appears now in bodies, engraved in them and at the same time subordinated to them – all the more as we consider activities such as research or software, where work does not crystallize in a material product separate from the worker but remains incorporated in the brain, indissociable from physical persons.[3] Here *fixed capital* is *social cooperation*. Here the boundaries of the relationship between living labour and dead labour (that is, between variable capital and fixed capital) are definitively put into crisis.

Thus the emancipatory functions of the cooperation of living labour invest and increasingly occupy the spaces of fixed capital.

More on this point – from Vercellone and Christian Marazzi: what is called immaterial or intellectual capital is in reality essentially incorporated in human beings, and therefore fundamentally corresponds to the intellectual and creative faculties of labour power. Consequently we can recognize it as the social individual. We find ourselves, as anticipated, in a situation of upheaval of the very concepts of constant capital and organic composition of capital that we inherited from industrial capitalism. In the ratio of constant capital (C) to variable capital (V), which designates mathematically the social organic composition of capital, it is in fact V, labour power, that appears as the principal fixed capital and – to adopt Marazzi's expression – as the 'machine body' of 'labour power'. This is because, as Marazzi points out, 'in addition to containing the faculty of labour, it also acts as a container of the typical functions of fixed capital and of the means of production qua sedimentation of codified knowledge, historically acquired knowledges, productive grammars, experiences – in short, past labour'.[4]

Now, for the revolutionary rupture to take place within this framework, the social individual has to be transformed into a political force.

People will say: how can you imagine that the most exploited, the precarious and the marginalized cognitive workers, can form this power? I believe that they can, because the full force of the production and reproduction of life is in their hands. How it can come about, I don't know. But I am working to make it happen. I have never understood why domination should be given as something that cannot be reversed, why the destiny of subjection should be taken to be necessary – and all the more when labour power is subsumed under general intellect and its high cognitive value, when the dignity of labour develops in cooperation, when labour power presents itself as the potential of the social individual.

Social individual: this is the current name of *the working class*. Movements of struggle, of social rejection of exploitation are multiplying. So we have to imagine what it means for this subject in struggle to renew the soviets, in other words to bring force, the multitude, and the common within the present realities of production and to overthrow the new totalitarian organizations of money and finance. The multitudinous *social individual* is socially exploited, as the worker was once in the factory. *Mutatis mutandis*, the validity of the class struggle is now confirmed at the social level. Capital, let us always remember, is an antagonistic relation of force between those who command and those who work. Now, that is where the rupture may occur. According to one of our anarcho-communist comrades, a great connoisseur of the digital world, it can be done in two ways. One would be through the traditional struggle of the trade union, of the associations [*leghe*], and of coordinated grassroots committees – and this is a struggle that runs through the paths of cooperativism between platforms; it is an already existing movement, which seeks to digitize the mutualistic structures of the welfare state and to create political alternatives to the current capitalist platforms. The second would be the path of digital commons, which create the material and economic conditions for reaching the truly communist potential of the platforms and discovering their true nature: the overcoming of private property, the abolition of wage labour and the creation of the government of common goods.[5]

The key assumption here is the recognition that labour is not capital: it is rather a revolutionary force, productive of freedom and of commonality.

Part III

Polemical Considerations

8

Operai e capitale Fifty Years On*

What Has Happened in the Working Class since Marx?

Antonio Negri and Mario Tronti

What has happened in the working class since Marx?

by Toni Negri

The first edition of *Operai e capitale* [*Workers and Capital*], in 1966, ended with a commitment to study '*what has happened within the working class since Marx*'.[1] The postscript to the second edition, published in 1970, analyses the working class in the New Deal and describes the transformations of technical composition (Fordism) and political composition (trade unionism and reformism, from the New Deal to the welfare state). However, regarding the working class, Tronti does not recognize a structural difference in technical and political composition between Fordism and the 1970s. There is no modification of labour processes; Taylorism and Keynesianism remain hegemonic; and class political relations are still dominated by the planner state. But between the first and the second edition of

* Paper presented at the University of Paris X Nanterre, 11 June 2016; published in EuroNomade under the title 'Operai e capitale: 50 anni' (visit http://www.euronomade.info/?p=7366). The seminar, titled 'Actualités d'ouvriers et capital', was part of a study day on Mario Tronti's book *Workers and Capital* and was held on the fiftieth anniversary of its publication. Participants included Andrea Cavazzini, Fabrizio Carlino, Yann Moulier Boutang, Etienne Balibar, and Morgane Mertueil. Antonio Negri made a spoken contribution and Mario Tronti contributed by means of a letter. Here we publish the text by Negri and the letter by Tronti. They indicate two different readings of the past fifty years, and also two ways of interpreting the present.

Operai e capitale we had the events of May '68. Yet Tronti seemed to think that not much had happened. The working class in 1968 and afterwards (in particular the Italian Hot Autumn) is still presented by him as being entirely within Fordism and the New Deal. In my opinion, Tronti was simultaneously right and wrong to take this position.

On the surface the situation seemed to be the same; the labour process had not changed. But, looking deeper, one thing was indeed changing, and 1968 was a symptom of it too. What was changing was the capital relation, the form of production processes, the mode of production. The year 1968 had begun this transformation. And Tronti was again right when, with much caution, he ventured in his 1970 postscript that a new phase was unfolding at the end of the long era of Fordism. Whereas in the Fordist period workers and capital had clashed within capital, now there was a new situation: working class and capital clashed within the working class. Tronti proposed to study this transition. It was a correct intuition. If one put aside the illusion, cultivated by some, that 'within the working class' meant 'within the Communist Party', one had to recognize that, in the new relationship of antagonism after 1968, capital paid for the passing of Fordism and the difficult victory achieved over the Fordist working class with an obligation to establish the axis of its command within the working class and to restructure its own project of accumulation inside there – thus undergoing a radical change in its structure. 'Within the working class' meant recognising – and this included *capital itself* – that 'the first principle [is] the struggle of the working class' and that, 'at the level of socially developed capital, capitalist development is subordinate to working-class struggles; not only does it come after them, but it must make the political mechanism of capitalist production respond to them' (*Workers and Capital*, p. 65); in other words, *capital* had to understand, at last, that its own technical composition (this being the Marxian concept of the organic composition of capital) needed to be modified in order to function (i.e. to produce and command) in the situation of a new political composition of the working class. In the process there had been something of an upheaval. The Trilateral Commission, for example, called it '68; others did not. But the fact was that a radical change had been imposed on capital. This had to do with the space of production (the physical location of production changed) and the dimension of temporality (the working day was radically transformed).

It was a real paradigm shift in the model of exploitation, and it had been produced by the working-class victory inside Fordism and against it. That the paradigm introduced by this victory was new is demonstrated by the fact that the antagonism of the 'capital relation' appeared – or, better, reopened – in new forms, which were to be experimented with, and within a new perspective of struggle for organization on both the capitalist side and the workers' side.

Let me now ask whether *Workers and Capital* offered the tools for describing this new structural paradigm. I would say yes. It seems to me that the essay 'Marx: Labour Power: Working Class' is foundational from this point of view. Taking that as a starting point, we were able to develop an analysis of capitalist development after 1968 that was very dynamic, because it highlighted the processes of subjectivation of the labouring class.

It is known that capital is a relation, a relationship, an antagonism of forces. Tronti has strongly insisted on the distinction between work and labour power. 'In the concept of *labour power* there is the figure of the worker, whereas this is not true of the concept of *labour*' (p. 111). And he finds that the seed of this political concept of labour power as non-capital develops throughout Marx's youthful writings: already in the *Manuscripts of 1844* Marx concludes this approach, proposing solutions that are immediately subversive. During the 1960s, when it was fashionable all across the board from right and left to separate the utopianism of Marx's youth from his thinking in *Capital*, Tronti pushes, on the contrary, for a close connection. Here, in this continuity of Marx's thought between youth and maturity, in the interweaving of philosophical and historical writings, and between all of these and *Capital*, one finds a political concept of labour power that functions as a picklock for every theoretical solution.

Secondly, this trend of research becomes even clearer in the analysis contained in the *Grundrisse*, which Tronti treats as the text of origin for *Capital*. Here the 'dual character' of labour power, that of being both a commodity and a subject, is spelled out powerfully. 'The only opposite to reified labour is unreified labour, subjective labour' (p. 157) – says Tronti, quoting from the *Grundrisse*, and this subjectivation is represented as the very condition of capital's existence.

In the *Grundrisse* – 'the internal monologue that Marx built up with himself, in his own time' (p. 212) – labour as subjectivity becomes central: 'If it is to be present in time, present alive, it can only be present as a living subject, in which it exists as capacity, as potentiality; therefore as worker' (p. 213). The dual character of the labour commodity is subjectivized, labour becoming on the one hand 'absolute poverty' – that is, total commodification of productive power – and on the other 'subjectivity', continuous subjectivation, and the general possibility of wealth as subject. The dual character of the labour power commodity is pushed to internalize itself to the maximum in capital:

> This is the new path that Marx himself here proposes. The starting point: labour as non-capital, and thus labour as the living subject of the worker as against the dead objectivity of all the other conditions of production; labour as the vital ferment of capital – another active determination added to the activity of productive labour. The point of arrival: capital, which itself becomes productive, an essential relation to the development of labour as a social productive power, and thus an essential relation to the *development* of the working class. . . . Along this path, between these two points, is labour as non-value, and, for this very reason, a living source of value; absolute misery and, for this very reason, a general possibility of wealth; again, surplus-labour and, for this very reason, surplus-value – the modern figure of the collective worker that now comes to produce capital precisely as an antagonistic class that combats it. (*Workers and Capital*, pp. 217–18)

> And what then needs doing, on this basis, is to set off in discovery of the working class's political laws of movement, which materially subordinate the development of capital to the working class itself. Thus will be found the definitive theoretical task, from the working class point of view. (*Workers and Capital*, p. 222)

Thirdly, according to Tronti, we are given here Marx's movement beyond the law of value – or rather a redefinition of it: 'Marx rejected the idea that labour is the source of all wealth and assumes a concept of labour as a measure of value' (p. 225). 'Labour value, then, means first labour-power, and then capital; it means capital conditioned by labour-power, moved by labour-power, value measured by labour. Labour is the measure of value because the working class is the condition of capital' (p. 228; translation modified). Needless to add, with this, the law of value is recognized for what it is: 'it cannot in fact be extrapolated from the capitalist relationship of production and from the class relation at the former's foundation' (p. 229). Wanting to become law, value, as a pure measure of value, transforms its action into mystification: by absolutizing itself, the law of value closes the *Trennung* [separation] between class and capital, perversely leading the capital relation to identity. Here – and this is not a negligible subject – the socialist ideology (and not only the Stalinist one) is definitively unmasked. And of it,

of the *objective economic functioning* of the labour-value law, we can
[paradoxically or scandalously: my addition] speak of this precisely
– and only – with reference to the very society that claims to have real-
ised ; socialism . . . we have to find the courage of our convictions and
recognise as a real historical fact the absurdity that the political power
of capital can take the form of a workers' state. (*Workers and Capital*,
p. 230)

Thus far we have seen the extent and depth of labour power's
internalization in capital. But the fact that the concept of capital is
a relation of force between dead labour accumulated in capital and
living labour, labour power, and its subjectivation means that this
relationship is an open field. The double character of labour power,
which we have seen acting in the submission to capital, can re-emerge
against the subordination to capital. It is from this starting point that
a sort of way up begins that is reconstructive, being supported by the
communist instance of the class struggle.

How can this revolutionary reopening of the capital relation
happen? The first precondition is the socialization of the productive forces, and this transition of the socialization of labour power
takes place completely within capital. Thus 'the productive power
developed by the labourer when working in cooperation is the productive power of capital' (p. 133). When 'a considerable number
of workers – which is to say, the workers socially combined within
one and the same process of production under the same capitalist
– become productive power for capital' (p. 133), then the rupture
becomes possible; but only possible. Here it is necessary to follow the
historical transition that 'on the working-class side of things . . . sees
first a seller of labour-power, then the individual productive power,
and then the social productive power' (p. 136). But what is labour
power constituted within capital? What does it mean to establish the
possibility of its being against capital? It means redeveloping without
interruption the antagonistic dynamic specific to the capital 'relation', its different balances – or, if you want to put it in the words of
another author dear to me, the 'civil war' that runs through the power
relationship. This possibility exists, obviously, on condition of not
'[fixing] the concept of the working class . . . in a single and definitive
form without development or history' (p. 135). Tronti adds that an
internal history of capital is emerging within the Marxist movement,
albeit with many difficulties:

But what is still far from being assumed as a programme of work –
or indeed as a principle of our research method – is the idea of an

> internal history of the working class, such as would reconstruct the
> moments of its formation, the changes in its composition, the growth
> of its organisation, according to the various successive determinations
> that labour-power assumes *qua* power producing capital, according to
> the diverse, recurrent and ever-new experiences of struggle that the
> working-class mass chooses *qua* the only antagonist of capitalist society.
> (*Workers and Capital*, p. 135)

It is therefore within the internal history of the working class that
Tronti's notion of 'within and against' should be analysed (pp. 133,
135). Here we have a founding moment of *operaismo* [workerism].
Three conditions for it are established at the base of every possibility
of a strategic overturning of the relations of production. The first two
conditions are those on which I have thus far dwelt extensively: the
subjectivation of labour power when, within the system of capital, it
has matured to the point where it

> really can be counted twice: one time as a force that produces capital
> and another time as a force that refuses to produce it; one time within
> capital, another time against capital. When the two times are subjec-
> tively unified on the working-class side, the route is opened to dissolve
> the capitalist system and the practical process of the revolution begins.
> (*Workers and Capital*, p. 173)

This is the third condition.

This is the crucial point of the workerist method – the point where
it becomes an oppositional genealogy in the internal history of both
class and capital. Marx's example of the English workers' struggle
for the reduction of the working day, a victorious struggle that introduces a new form of value creation (from absolute surplus value to
relative surplus value), is central here. The transformation of capital
is imposed in the very moment in which the composition of the
working class in struggle changes. Analysing this period of struggles,
Tronti stresses that 'a real political leap' has taken place here and
that one can speak of political 'cause' or 'effect' even when there is
no organized movement but only resistance, when there are elements
that are destituent and not yet explicitly political and constituent. In
fact the relationship between labour and capital no longer shows up
simply at the exchange in the labour market, as it did at the beginning of capitalism; it shows up within the production of capital and
exposes with great force how the figure of capital is determined by
the class relationship. And it is through this recognition that working-
class initiative becomes political. Tronti's example is still the old

example of the French workers' insurrection in 1848; and he repeats Marx's narrative, insisting on the fact that the transition from action for the overthrow of bourgeois society becomes a struggle for the overthrow of the form of the state. It is within these struggles that the transformation of the 'proletarian' into 'worker' – of the seller of labour power into producer of surplus value – gets organized, and it is here that a class in arms against the whole society transforms the relations of production into resistance, struggle and insurrection against these very relations.

Tronti observes that the struggle for the regulated working day preceded, imposed, and caused a change in the form of surplus value, a revolution in the mode of production, and this happened in Marx's *Capital* as well as in the very history of capitalist development. But here one can also note how a victory in the class struggle – in this case, the working class's imposition, on capital, of a specific interest – prefigures and overdetermines an interest (and a power) of capital; and this is not something exceptional in the history of capitalist development. But the model this time is not so much one of struggle as one of end of struggle; and it would recur in different forms, at different levels of development. And all this will continue: whenever the workers win a partial battle, they realize at a later stage that they won it for capital. Sometimes the class suffers terrible defeats, which force the movement to bend, but then it buckles down, re-emerging even stronger than before. Within these defeats, however, the transformation of the mode of production and the modification of the forms of surplus value mature and manifest themselves. The composition of the working class also changes as a result, as we have already seen. Even the name 'working class' can fail: not because the antagonistic structure of the working class has dissolved, but because the forms in which it produces and struggles have been transformed. Proletariat, working class, multitude: they do not represent opposing figures, they represent variable but homogeneous faces of a compound of resistances and of struggle in movement.

Today we witness a radical transformation of labour processes and of capital's mode of production. A labour power that is now socialized, precarious and global proposes a new terrain of struggle, namely in the 'new mode of production'. Work has become cognitive, affective, cooperative. The new mode of production was imposed by the workers' struggles of the last century – they produced it through the refusal of wage labour and the destruction of the centrality of the factory, and especially through two processes that accompany the development of cognitive capital: the workers' appropriations of an autonomous management of knowledges and of the processes of productive cooperation. Here the class struggle really begins to grow within the working class and the subjectivation of labour power begins to change (to put it like Tronti) into the power of the worker [*la potenza dell'operaio*]: in other words, subjectivation is determined through the incorporation of quotas of 'fixed capital' (knowledges and organization of work), which at other times were an instrument of capital's command over labour power. It is in response to those struggles that capital built its organization, which is based on the exploitation of the social power of labour and on the extraction of the common. This situation requires new strategies of movement in the struggle for communism and seeks new tactics of organization. But, as far as the method and the axiomatics of research are concerned, we remain on the solid ground proposed by Tronti in *Workers and Capital*. If there is any difference between workerism and post-workerism – *if* indeed there is any difference – it lies in class knowledge, that is, in the recognition of the historical transformation of the production relation and of the subject that is exploited in it. But at the same time it forces capital to suffer a new effect of resistance and struggle, of hatred and hope.

To conclude, let me look at an example of method, which operates in the presence of a new composition of labour – cognitive workers – and of the terrible conditions of precariousness and unemployment to which they are subjected. Capital would very willingly continue to let these new generations of workers die, were it not to risk the deterioration of these precious productive capacities and the blockage of the new forms of social accumulation, through the extraction of the common. So then, what will it do? The first hypothesis, that of killing [*far morire*], is one that we experience every day on the frontiers of Europe, the United States and in the lower Pacific – and also, randomly, in our daily lives. But capitalist 'rationality' – always a function of accumulation – will impose another choice. Capital will rather be obliged to develop forms of social salarization and to reshape the institutions of welfare in order to control the dynamics of resistance and to exercise domination. Wage measures ('citizen income', for example) and welfare measures can be a matter of mix and match in the capitalist management of change; what matters is that they keep a balance between workers' productivity and their lives and do so at the lowest possible cost.

But here things become complicated on both the capitalists' side and the workers' side. Regarding the former, it is incumbent upon them to reorganize the internal arrangements in order to absorb and regulate, as well as to impose an orderly accumulation of new social flows of value – because the transformation of the mode of production brings about new forms of surplus value (the social one after the absolute and the relative ones) and imposes new hierarchies on capitalist command – in this case, financial. For the workers, too, many things change: the working day, which is now without a temporal measure, the workplace, which has become mobile and transferable, and also the form of the wage, which has been socialized and is fixed at the lowest ratio between primary income and welfare services. Well, all this definitively destroys forms and traditions of struggle; nevertheless, it also configures a new social terrain of organization and of anticapitalist motions. Let us ask ourselves, would it be a victory for the working class, to obtain a citizen income articulated to the needs provided by welfare? Or would this simply be a new way of organizing labour power as 'variable capital'? Obviously, both. But on this basis there could be – and this is what interests me – a new terrain of struggle, and therefore a possibility of organization for cognitive workers. And they, given the rich quality of their composition, cannot limit their initiative to the terrain of pure resistance. 'Schumpeter portrays the figure of the entrepreneur with his innovating initiative; it is pleasing for us to see this figure turned inside out, as the permanent initiative-in-struggle of the great masses of the working class' (p. 212). All right; but now we have new compositions, both technical and political, much more productive than at that time, and far larger multitudes, and consequently a greater possibility of constructing transitions that are constitutive of a new social order. This is what we have been seeing and studying since 2011.

Is there too much optimism in this foundation and in this revival of the workerist method? Is it as if the defeat of the 1970s – a defeat of those who had refused the peaceable return into the arms of the Italian Communist Party – were not accorded the great seriousness that it had? Do we not encounter here, again, the illusion that the multitude at work, as a plural set of singularities, can miraculously regroup? To put it in philosophical terms, is there not a poor ontological hypostasis – not so much in the revival of the workerist method as in the redefinition of a subject in struggle? These objections, which are frequently brought against the workerists, seem to me to be unacceptable. First, because the methodology of *Workers and Capital*, at the encounter with Tronti's political hypothesis, was (and has been) practised completely independently of any reduction to unity and party transcendence, and is thus saved from the kind of vanguardist insurrectional machination that is so characteristic of socialist eschatology. So much so that the workerist hypothesis has been a natural gathering place for the theoretical, historiographical and political experiences that have made the autonomous movements from below the key to all the more recent instances of revolutionary practice, from 'another world is possible' [*altermondialisti*] movements at the turn of the century to the ones that have spread all over the world since 2011. Secondly, any finalistic hypothesis and any unitary telos are excluded from this implant – and I mean the diagnostic implantation of the theory that some call 'post-workerist' (if this is the one that subjectivizes the multitudinous singularities and considers the cognitive workforce implanted in the common). Subjective intentionality cannot be confused with teleological determinism. If there is a 'progressive field' produced by struggles, it is the one built through the strength of the movements. There is no destiny other than the discontinuous one we build, and our freedom always has the mark of that necessity. This, too, is what we learned from the workerism of *Workers and Capital*.

Dear comrades

by Mario Tronti

Dear comrades, thank you for this tribute to a bygone event. Fifty years, half a century: this is the distance since then. It's a long time. 'Actualités' ['Points of Relevance'], you say, of *Workers and Capital*; in the plural. So is there, could there be, more than one? Or at least something that is different, alongside so many non-*actualités*? On the other hand, ever since Nietzsche, there is a lot of ambiguity between and the actual and the non-actual. Which is it better to be? Then, at the age of thirty, I perceived myself (and wanted) to be actual more than I perceive myself (and want) to be non-actual today, in my mid-eighties.

Workerism was an intense and beautiful experience; a formative experience for young antagonistic minds that has bequeathed a knowledge of presence and struggle, handed down through successive generations to the present day, perhaps with a unique creative continuity. That was a sign that the seed was good, and so was the ground on which it fell, in places where even today, after many huge changes, it sprouts in spite of everything. I have a fine and vivid memory of that heroic age, of that practice of conflict, of that way of thinking, of that choice of action, of that form of writing that is no longer to be found, because it was completely dictated by the immediate need to act, and to act in a direct interface with the world, without mediations and concessions. Above all, I have a great nostalgia for those people, those men and women engaged in acting and in a collective feeling, where the authenticity of being, and of being there, brought into existence a human surplus value that, I confess, in the long years and decades that followed, sadly I have not been able to recognize around me.

The 1960s and 1970s were our 'twenty glorious years'. There the revolutions of the twentieth century came to an end. An age of restoration opened up, which is still under way. And then came the desert. In the two wastelands that I was given to inhabit, that of university academia and that of politicking politics, there was room only for a hermit monk's cell. There began a difficult path of thinking and acting: advances, turns, stops, backtrackings. First of all it was necessary to keep the journey on track, to create makeshift compass readings in the absence of cardinal points of reference: in practice, this was an antagonistic political realism. The mysterious curve of Lenin's line seemed to me the one that suited me best. The linear path had been interrupted. The whole progress of humanity towards something better had crashed into a wall, and one that was not as easy to break down as ideological walls. There was no other way than to take the curve, taking care not to skid. We still place ourselves at the point of maximum expansion of this curved line. Beyond the skirmishes at the borders of the empire or empires, we are inside a new hundred years' peace. We complain about the degradation of the political classes, the corruption of the institutions, the silence of the classes in the disappearance of the class struggle, and the anthropological drift into a malaise of civilization. When you have lived seventy years of peace, all this is bound to happen. I am saying that this is not about lowering the level of opposition to an inimical reality, but about seeking, with the same passion as in the past, the most suitable, namely contemporaneous, forms of thought and action. The philosophy of practice has failed, has broken into two. And the levels of critique and intervention have to be managed in two different ways. The concise synthetic formula 'long thinking, short action' guided and still guides me in my daily navigation through the becalmed realities of today's oceans.

Today, as far as I am concerned, this is the path that must be laid down, and above all understood. What has to be subjected to critique is the whole period that followed the direct confrontation between workers and capital. What remains of the first workerism, of which

Workers and Capital is only an expression? Some things remain, such as the ones mentioned in the posting for the Nanterre conference: the partisan point of view from which to address everything – that remains; the conflictual conception of the social relationship – that remains; the subjectivity of struggles that imposes the terrain of the initiative on the opponent – that remains. But what remains for me above all is the political reading of the class struggle, the anti-economicism, the anti-sociologism, the anti-ideologism. It is what brings me today to support this idea, manifestation of an extreme thought: that, in order to break down the threat of working-class centrality, capitalism had to break down the centrality of industry, which consequently led to this new form of capitalist order based on financial disorder, where the periodic crisis no longer interrupts the ongoing development but, on the contrary, the periodic development interrupts the permanent crisis. When I say this, I see the wide-eyed looks of economists, be they neoliberals, post-Keynesians or pseudo-Marxists. Is this thesis true? Is it not true? I don't care. I am not looking for a historical truth that is objective and good for all inorganic intellectuals. I am looking for a forceful political idea, which I need in order to build a battlefront that goes to the root of the current social divisions. This is living workerist thinking. If one puts it like this, one could derive a content for that beautiful formula about the 1 per cent and the 99 per cent, which otherwise risks being ideologically empty. If one puts it like this, a left that had declared itself heir to the great history of the labour movement could have had a reason for being and an opportunity for recognition among all those excluded from wealth and power. The 'irrational' core of workerism was not a minority point of view. On the contrary, it was potentially form and matter for a new logic of the world, antagonistic to the dominant one, ready to devastate the twenty-first century.

My dearest friends, these last expressions are easily recognizable. I really appreciate, but at the same time I am not convinced, when Dardot and Laval return to talking about the concept of revolution. We can't talk about it between Arendt and Castoriadis. There can be no reasoning between the 1776 revolution and the 1789 revolution in the absence of the 1917 revolution, whose centenary we shall celebrate next year. We cannot say 'common' without saying 'communism'. I continue to be convinced that the communists are the only ones who really have struck fear into the capitalists. It wasn't the social democrats, the liberals, the anarchists, the terrorists of '68: it was us, the workerists. Those other things only tickled the system. Only the (tragic) attempt at a communist construction of socialism gave them a punch in the stomach that put them for decades in a state of worried defence of their order, between the great crisis and the great war. Ever since the failure of that attempt, they have had no more problems, apart from the ones that they themselves create, among themselves. I am glad that Toni rereads his personal history, which I always follow with militant passion, as the story of a communist. It is a highly demanding statement of possession. It should be taken on board in all its historical richness. It often happens, in these miserable times that we are living, that I find myself reminding people, especially for the sake of those who are to come in the future, of the need for a jealous cultivation of memory. I seem to see more revolutionary chances in our past, which no one can take away from us, than in a future that has already been taken from us, that is by now entirely in the hands of those in power. We are in the grip of this terrible vice: never has another world been more necessary than it is today, and never has that other world been more impossible than it is today. We say: it is not possible for the moment. We do not know how long this moment is going to be. Here the theoretical–historical concept of revolution returns. I am taken by an idea, which I would like to find the time to process. The revolution is not the act with which one takes power, but the process by which one manages power. Reformers first, and revolutionaries only afterwards. I leave you with this flash of lightning without thunder.

9

On Tronti's Autonomy of the Political*

I must confess to a measure of embarrassment in discussing this volume of writings by Mario Tronti that gives an overview of his life as a scholar and a militant. When I was young – well, not that young: around the age of thirty – Mario taught me to read Marx. This was a big undertaking, and I'm still grateful to him for it. It was on the basis of this reading that I dedicated myself to a militant life. But six or seven years after that opening, in 1966, when he delivered to us his *Workers and Capital*,[1] Mario left us – and I don't say 'me' but 'us', because in the meantime so many workerists [*operaisti*] had come to be present not only in universities but especially in the large factories of northern Italy. He told us that year that the decade of the 1960s had ended before its time and, with it, the period of working-class autonomy, so that we had to find a higher level for the struggles we had conducted and were still conducting; we had to bring the struggle into the Italian Communist Party (PCI). Wasn't that what we were already doing? – we replied. Neither then nor later were we insensitive to the problem and to the task of developing politically the workers' struggles. The fact is that the party did not like it at all. In the acceleration of workers' struggles that would take us to 1968–9, we did not understand then why we should leave the autonomy of struggles to itself. Mario then said that '68 had definitely confused us. In his opinion, we had taken for a dawn what was in fact a sunset. But what sunset? Certainly we were coming to the end of the hegemony

* Speech given by Toni Negri at the presentation of Mario Tronti's book *Il demone della politica* [*The Demon of Politics*] at the Sorbonne, Paris, 5 April 2019; published in EuroNomade under the title 'Sull'autonomia del politico di Tronti' on 12 April 2019 (http://www.euronomade.info/?p=11933).

of the mass worker, but could that be confused with the end of the proletarian class struggle? As the long Italian 1968 extended through the entire 1970s, Mario's conversion did not convince us. That was when I stopped reading Tronti. When this present volume arrived, I realized that I had read only the first third of it; there were still two thirds for me to read.

Of course, even if I wasn't reading him, Tronti was not absent from my daily reality. He was present in an irritating manner – for example, during those years I read an essay on the history of modern political thought that Mario had just published and that, to the Spinozist I was becoming, seemed partisan and certainly not pleasing in its unreserved exaltation of Hobbes's theory of power. It was as if the history of modern politics should not be traversed also by the thinking and history of those who had been defeated, by the line of rebellion, by the communist dream, before it comes to be represented in Marx as a critique of political economy and as a potential of classist subjectivation. I was deeply attached to this figure of the history of the modern and it was specifically from *Workers and Capital* that I had learned to pursue the internal history of the working class – the story of its progressive becoming subject. I did this by developing Tronti's intuition about the point at which the subjectivation of labour power had matured so that 'the same productive force really can be counted twice: one time as a force that produces capital and another time as a force that refuses to produce it; one time within capital, another time against capital' (p. 173). Why then, I asked myself, does Mario in his historical work forget the struggle against capital and the powerful subjectivation of the proletariat?

Then again, during those years it made me angry when Cacciari and Asor Rosa, following Mario's line, attacked Foucault, because – they said – he dissolved the state, which was the object and the subject of their conception of politics. It was then that, probably for the first time, I came to realize fully that the political terrain chosen by my old comrades was given exclusively as a statist apparatus and was detached, radically separated from the level of the class struggle. What an incredible limitation this was – and also from the point of view offered to us by Foucault, whose concept of power resonated so powerfully with the dualism of Marx's concept of capital!

Then, in more recent times, I wondered in perplexity what exactly workerism [*operaismo*] meant, having heard people call me a 'post-workerist' when instead I had taken up the theoretical task of expanding the methodological techniques and political intuitions of the 'crude' workerism of the 1960s via an analysis of the transformation of class composition and class struggle at the international level. In the global knowledge market I very much wanted to be defined as a 'workerist': I am not ashamed to say it, and I was happy to leave the 'post-' part to those who in reality had taken another direction. I was certainly in a minority, but, as often happens to minorities, I felt that soon enough the state-oriented party options of those who really came after the (post-)workerists would be broken in the rebirth of the class struggle.

However, to avoid these increasingly frequent feelings of anger, I told myself finally that I really ought to go and hear Mario again. I was in prison at the time, and in 2001 Mario was giving the final lecture of his academic career in Siena. I asked the prison authorities for an exit permit and, surprisingly, they granted it. I saw Siena again, after so many years of exile, and this fact was not entirely unconnected to my request to travel to listen to Mario. The title of Mario's lecture was 'Politics and Destiny'. I realized then how far our ways had parted. I knew well the young Hegel's fragment on freedom and destiny, already translated into Italian and commented upon by Cesare Luporini, that Mario took as a starting point of his study – I had worked on it in my thesis. So what became of that highly republican text of the young Hegel in Mario's reading of it? He operated an unprecedented shift from Hegel's *Bestimmung* [destiny] to Heidegger's *Geschick* [fate], from Hegel's ethical–political determination and revolutionary reliance on popular *Begeisterung* [enthusiasm] – from this, then – to Heidegger's decision to abandon the being in Being. But why this step? How could this shift from Hegelian enthusiasm to deadly Heideggerianism have occurred? The answer turned out to be highly metaphorical. It came in the form of an awareness of the definitive crisis of a political destiny staked entirely on membership in the Communist Party. But at that time, in 2001, the party was no longer there. Why? Mario answered that question metaphorically: '*Perché non c'è più popolo*' – 'Because the people no longer exists.'

I wondered, what was this hegemonic mythology that made Mario react so dramatically and – in my opinion – so disastrously, in the face of the present reality of the class struggle? Herein lies Tronti's enigma; but it does not seem to me too difficult to unravel. It is a dislocation of point of view – from within and against capital to within the Party, with the idea of imposing its hegemony on capitalist development; it is a profound discontinuity between the Tronti of *Workers and Capial* and the Tronti of the 'autonomy of the political'. Put simply, it is a shift of the source of power and initiative of class struggle *from the bottom to the top*.

The concept of autonomy of the political first saw the light of day in 1972, in a piece of writing of this title. It was no longer the residue of a historical tradition, of a Hobbesian memory. The concept was organized rather on the idea that it was necessary to have done with Marxian 'monotheism', that is, with the claim that the critique of political economy and the critique of politics could derive from the same source. Instead, according to Mario, these were two different critical practices. Politically, this duplication was justified – not entirely paradoxically – by the idea that in the 1970s capitalism had proved to be insufficient to support the modern state, in other words capitalist development in the form of the modern state. But if capitalism falls behind, it is politics that has to shake it up. Politics needs to be urged to modernize the state. But 'politics' today is only the strength of the class organized in the party. Who, then, should be in charge of modernizing the state? 'The working class', which 'is in this respect the only true rationality of the modern state'.[2] Here the paradox becomes total.

The working class as 'rationality of the modern state': the phrase is hard to justify, either vis-à-vis the 'crude' workism of the early 1960s or if we look ahead, to the fate of the class and of the modern state. For, in the first case, workerist rationality had represented precisely the opposite of a progressive function of capitalist development; if it caused capitalist development, it did so as an antagonistic agent and by no means as an instrumental agent, let alone as a rational function. In the second case – looking ahead to the development of the dialectic between class struggle and state, one can say that it emptied itself out during the following decades and in the form metaphorized by Tronti – in the sense that the class, when it acts as an antagonistic and propulsive force of capital, will never again be represented by the party.

But let me get back to us, to 1972. Tronti recognizes that this political autonomy can be taken as a directly capitalist political project. In this case, he concedes, it would turn out to be the last of the bourgeois ideologies. However, at the time, in the 1970s, it was still feasible as a workerist claim. 'The modern state is, at this point, nothing less than the modern form of autonomous organization of the working class.'[3] The relationship is perfected a decade later, under Enrico Berlinguer, when the historical compromise is put on the agenda. I say 'perfected' because it is accompanied by a further underestimation of the revolutionary role of the working class. Theoretically, as Mario puts it, '[t]he working class, on the basis of the struggle within the production relationship, is only occasionally able to win. Strategically it does not win; strategically it is a class that remains dominated; but if it does not stake itself simply on the terrain of class, if it steps out and takes hold of the political terrain, then there are moments when the process of capitalist domination can be overturned.' Here we have the full expression of the break with the workerism of the 1960s.

In the discussion (that text on the autonomy of the politics came to be elaborated into a discussion document) the thesis is attenuated; sometimes the dualistic relationship of capital theorized in *Workers and Capital* is reintroduced: 'In capitalist society there is never domination by a single class.'[4] We are in 1972 here, and I imagine that various interlocutors reminded Mario of the intensity of the struggles in progress. And here is how Tronti reacts: 'A capitalist development of this kind cannot advance unless it eliminates this state apparatus before it that no longer corresponds to the current level of capitalist economic development. This is the prediction that I make.'[5] Mario is of course right about this: it is the moment when capital opens up to the *global* reorganization of sovereignty. But this time 'big politics' eludes him. Indeed, Tronti still thinks that these are operations within the fabric of the nation-state, and adds naively: 'When capital decides to shift its action onto that terrain' – he has in mind, obviously the theme of state reform –

> the whole game of class struggle also shifts, of necessity, onto that terrain. In my opinion, one should anticipate the same capitalist move on this terrain, addressing the issue of political bottlenecks and therefore of reform of the state structure even before capital becomes aware of it and elaborates a project for the effective and concrete implementation of this reform. Thus the process, I would not say of reform, but of *political revolution of the capitalist state* as it is, is a project that the working class has to anticipate.

And here is the claim for the instrument of political autonomy: 'We find that there is a level of the labour movement, that is, a historical organization of the labour movement, that is available for an action of this kind.'[6] And again: 'For a project of this type, we have organizational tools that, by reason of past politics and their internal structure, are available for an action of this type. As a historical situation it is paradoxical, but it is a paradox to be used.' One could mock this supposed 'political realism' – but to what purpose, once we get the measure (as we can today) of the idealism that underpinned it?

The class must become state: this, therefore, is the autonomy of the political, as it appears again in Tronti's *Il Tempo della politica* [*The Time of Politics*] in 1980. This text is interesting. There is a degree of self-criticism about his verdict on 1968. For example, he recalls the working-class matrix of 1968, and even states that before 1968 there had been, at the European and international level, a victorious cycle of workerist struggles that prepared the way for it. Tronti exemplifies 'the Italian case', giving an account of the totality of processes that led the workers in struggle to come out of the factories. He even opens up to a first definition of the social as a new terrain of class struggle. And he inveighs against the party's inability to absorb and to dialecticize the new movements, which he attributes to slow reflexes, a fear of the new, and a tendency to self-preservation.[7]

But then, as if nothing had happened, he goes back to insisting that the party is the key to every process. What is literally unacceptable is that all this discourse is now premised on the elimination of any kind of critical approach to political economy, and supports itself on a bizarre voluntarism. 'Rosenzweig indicated a reading perspective for modern politics, *von Hegel zu Bismarck* [from Hegel to Bismarck]. Is it possible to draw the line further and continue the conversation and reshuffle the cards *von Bismarck zu Lenin* [from Bismarck to Lenin]? Only those who have no spirit of research can be shocked by this idea – those who are afraid that their ideas may get dirty by handling practices of the enemy, those who think small, along lines of ideological coherence, and not on the basis of the political productivity of a theoretical choice.'[8] Maybe. But I remind you that, after having tasted that passage through Bismarck, Franz Rosenzweig had opted for the mystical *Stern der Erlösung* (*The Star of Redemption*). Tronti will not be offended, because this is the very same path he himself will take.

I shall come back to this. But for the moment let me pursue the theme of the autonomy of the political. In 1998 Tronti declares the end of the phase of the autonomy of the political. Why does this phase come to an end? It comes to an end as a result of the defeat of the labour movement, which, according to him, is beyond possible recovery: it is dead, even if the working class is not. After the subordination of the class struggle to the autonomy of the political, the class struggle stops with the end of the PCI. *Quod erat demonstrandum*, I might add: he wanted to prove this, and to propose a further answer to the question about the end of the autonomy of the political – because Tronti's line of thought moves from every political error to a transcendental transfiguration of it (from the failure of 'the party in the factory' to the idea of the 'autonomy of the political', from the crisis of '68 to the affirmation of the class as state, from the failure of the historic compromise to political theology), in a headlong flight with no end. Tronti concedes that the revolts of the subordinated remain in their eternal course. As intended, his discourse now moves to the eternal: the God who becomes a human being and the human being who becomes God have not met, and serious doubts are formulated about the eleventh of Marx's theses on Feuerbach (i.e. 'Thus far philosophers have only interpreted the world; now the time has come to change it'). The 'dogma of practice' gets dismantled. The PCI has come to an end, and so has any kind of revolutionary politics. But so, too, has progressive and reformist politics. If it were not shouted so forcefully, this conviction could be expressed in a twilight tone and could order both the nostalgia (how many times recalled) of the 'communist people' [*il popolo comunista*] and the sense of new, incomprehensible times. A Pasolinian aura.

In the article 'Karl und Carl'[9] the discourse on the autonomy of the political reappears, but this time sublimated. Tronti gives it to us as 'the last thing left'. So the autonomy of the political is no longer connected to the history of the labour movement or its politics, but is finally given here as an ontological fact, as a necessity of thought, of life and of human coexistence. One could say, ironically, that it is no longer a mode but an attribute of being. Tronti acknowledges that, for the workerists who entered the PCI in the 1970s, the genuine circumstance of the encounter with Schmitt was produced in the beginning 'by the practical ambition to gather from Schmitt the secret of political autonomy, to deliver it as an offensive weapon to the working class party'.[10] This confirms precisely the hypothesis I formulated before. But, Tronti adds, it was necessary to go beyond contingency. It was necessary to recognize that a strategic step had been taken, in adopting from Schmitt (in his own words) the thought of the originality of the political, of politics as an original potentiality. The logic could not be more consequential. A new monotheism had been built, opposed to the monotheism denounced in Marx.

What is there to say about the rest of this book? I can say that it often loses sight of political judgements on present realities in the middle of spiritual, theological and transcendental whispers. Power becomes definitively dehistoricized. The theological–political takes over. The sense of the religious appears in the tone of a nihilism that follows from the declaration of the end of modern political language and of its world – an end coterminous with that of the twentieth century. We are facing a catastrophic, unstoppable decline. Now everything is the same, and the function of political thought can only be a katechontic one: to block that decline, to slow it down.

It honestly makes me sad that *Workers and Capital*'s original attempt to regain the political through the subjectivation of the proletarian actor in the class struggle ends up in a sad commiseration of human 'virtue'. This had crossed paths with 'fortune' and so, in the party, it was in our power not only save ourselves from ruin but also to build a new world. But once 'fortune' fails, any 'virtue' declines with it. How un-Machiavellian this destiny is. In the writings of Machiavelli, the fortune that disappears is, at least in latency, a bearer of new virtue. Such is the situation today. And a genetically robust thought like that of Tronti should not have lost the ability to notice it: yes, the end of the party is indeed the end of an era, but it also signals the birth of new subjectivations.

Lamenting the defeat produces an idle metaphysical flight, renewed – when what is needed is a laborious but positive folding into the critique of political economy, a new set of questions on the technical and political composition of the working class that, within these contingencies, is constituting itself into new figures. How have labour power and variable capital changed in their relation to fixed capital, within the changes of the capitalist mode of production and in the transition from the industrial to the postindustrial phase? What is that 'intellectuality' that constitutes the new multitude of workers, and what are the forms of its productive being? And the new centrality of cooperation in work, its heightened intensity in the sphere of labour – immaterial, cognitive, online, and so on – this powerful transversality, what consequences do they bring about? If the social worker [*operaio sociale*] becomes a cognitive worker [*lavoratore cognitivo*] and grafts linguistic and technological cooperation onto the former's qualities of mobility and flexibility, how can the relationship and the leap from technical to political composition of the new proletariat take place? If it is true that within this transformative turmoil the only thing that does not change is the fact that capital lives on surplus labour and continually reconfigures surplus value and profit within it, then that relationship between technical and political composition is possible; it is a latent *dispositif* to be developed and a task *to be performed.*

What is certain is that workerism needs to be brought up to date; and it can be, at a time when the socialization of production and cognitive labour imbue accumulation and the entire life. It is not by chance that feminist movements are becoming central in social reproduction and in life. Besides, the viewpoint of subalterns reveals completely its connection with class movements. Would it not be possible to reactualize here, in the new struggles of these subjects, the angle that originally created workerism – the understanding from below, from the optic of the class struggle of the exploited, of every historical development in the struggle for liberation *from* work? And, with it, the capacity to give this angle biopolitical intensity and universal extension? Is it not the case that, once the centrality of the factory is over, class struggle regains here fully its revolutionary potential?

I'll stop my questions here and I'll suggest what the hypothesis of a new political composition allows us to deduce from that inquiry into the new technical composition of the proletariat. Such a composition may come about when, in recognizing the productive excess of cooperative and cognitive labour that characterizes the phase of new accumulation, the working class rebels and shows itself capable of handling *in time* the rupture of the production relationship, of building a *counterpower*, and of establishing constituent legitimacy in this manner. Here the name of politics gets reattached to that of producing, not in an economistic sense but in the sense built by struggles: as free capacity to produce and to exercise command over life.

Finally, to conclude, I'll make a highly polemical point about Mario. *Pace* the claim he makes each time he articulates his theory of politics and power, the autonomy of the political has nothing to do with Lenin. For Lenin was indeed a monotheist, but in a sense opposite to Schmitt's: he also derived from Marx the idea of a political that, *in matter*, was made up essentially of the massified projection of living labour; *in form*, of a party organization based on the factory, on the productive community; and, *in project*, of a revolutionary effort of building the common. In Lenin there is no way of detaching matter from form. The reference often made here to the New Economic Policy, to show up Lenin as an opportunist realist, takes us to Stalinist policies to come rather than to Lenin's political model, whose dominant elements are abolition of the state, transition to a phase in which the proletariat reappropriates and transforms the powers of the state, and desire to create a classless society. True, in pressing ahead with his destruction of the communist tradition, Tronti dims this allocation of Lenin to the autonomy of the political. Tronti's self-critique (if only it were that! . . . it comes across instead as a higher power of truth) seems to change ground. After theory, mythology; after mysticism, asceticism. He claims that the Marxism of the twentieth century, in the form of Leninism, is very much a philosophy of mythology. However, this transformation is welcome. It was extremely dangerous to carry on with the idea of a Lenin devoted to the autonomy of the political, since this has strong overtones of historical revisionism. After 'Lenin equals Bismarck' comes 'Lenin equals Hitler', an idea that is entirely acceptable for Schmitt – but certainly not for us.

But the reference to the political transcendental, which was typical of twentieth-century statist pathology – that 'destructive wrath of Achilles, that brought countless woes upon the Achaeans'[11] – has had its day. In the globalized world, every statist reminiscence is destined to bow to sovereignism and to identitarianism and renews fascist tendencies, while the figure of the state pales in the context of globalization. Far from reappearing as an autonomous subject, the state assumes a subordinate role in the global game of profit rates. Other comrades, still workerists, have concluded that the state 'is not powerful enough to confront contemporary capitalism' and that 'a different source of power is necessary . . . that is not centered on the state but capable of combining the establishment of a system of social counterpowers with wider, transnational attempts to seize political spaces or even create new ones'.[12] This is where the workerist perspective, the one that Tronti gave us and that he has been rejecting for quite some time, can help us. So, if my reading of the volume stops at the end of its first third, it is not certain that precisely from there, from that first third, one might not proceed afresh to the discovery of the political in Marx.

10

Post-*operaismo*?*

No, Just *operaismo*!

In the Marxist theoretical literature of recent times, people often speak of *operaismo* [workerism] and post-*operaismo* [postworkerism]. As we know, *operaismo* was born in Italy in the late 1950s and found expression in the 1960s, in the journals *Quaderni rossi* and *Classe operaia*. There are doubts about the continuity of *operaismo* between that foundation and the 1970s, when it experienced a first phase of expansion, and then the twenty-first century, when it was incorporated into debate at an international level. Some have proposed that we should use the term '*operaismo*' to refer only to the raw *operaismo* of the 1960s, and to call the later phenomenon 'post-*operaismo*'. But does such a thing as post-*operaismo* really exist? If it does, it arises out of the debates, the philosophical readings and the sociological reflections of the militant *operaisti* [workerists] incarcerated in Italy's prisons during the 1980s, a time when they were trying to understand the defeat of working-class struggles at the onset of neoliberalism. So if post-*operaismo* has an origin, it is a noble one – associated with its emergence from the Resistance – and it is because of its capacity for understanding defeat and going beyond it that it has exerted an influence on the succession of social struggles for the common in the decades that bridge the two centuries.

Before asking whether one can actually speak of 'post-*operaismo*' as a method and a current of ideas distinct from those of *operaismo*, let me first try to understand how the problem has been framed, or how a misunderstanding has arisen around that 'post-'. What was

---

* Talk given at Gonville & Caius College, Cambridge, 25 April 2017; published in EuroNomade (http://www.euronomade.info/?p=9189).

operaismo in the 1960s? Put briefly, it was a theory of class struggle founded on a constituent ontology rather than on a dialectical ontology, on the subjectivation of living labour rather than on Hegelian dialectic, albeit overturned as in Marx. And by the way, let us not be afraid of the word 'ontology'. It designated exactly the priority of living labour with respect to capitalist domination – neither more nor less; the constitutive productivity of labour in the face of its exploitation; the intransitive asymmetry of living labour's relationship with dead labour. Now, in the prisons, after a decade of struggles, ontology comes to mean that we are nevertheless within a strong reality, within an ineradicable experience and a depth of resistance that was and remains irrepressible. The class struggle was there, impossible to suppress. The question was to bring the previous practices of class struggle up to date on the basis of an analysis of the new forms of exploitation. What people call 'post-*operaismo*' thus starts from a radical rereading of the form of value – that is, from the new social conditions in which neoliberalism's techniques of domination and the new resistance to exploitation develop – and it takes them as the basis of analysis.

There is, then, on the one hand a theoretical reflection on the value form, and this reflection is strongly influenced by a reading of the work of Isaak Rubin. There 'value form' meant that, when the magnitudes of value changed (and the law of labour value as a tool for measuring valorization went into crisis), and the substance of value – that is, the relationship that tied the quality of productive labour (now increasingly immaterial) to capitalist command – changed too, this led to a change in the overall shape of capital's domination. The inquiries, albeit uncompleted, into the becoming social of work and the consequent formation of a postindustrial order that was highlighted at that time by capitalist labour policies themselves, and also the advances made in the philosophical critique of capitalist totalization, against the Frankfurt School – a critique already put forward in the 1960s and now taken up and deepened in the wake of the French poststructuralists – now opened to a historically changing horizon, on which it was confirmed that the dialectic of the relation of capital could no longer work on the triadic rhythm of affirmation–negation–overcoming (or, in workerist jargon,* 'struggles–crisis–restructuring'). The rhythm of the capital relation had become linear; the capital relation now insisted on a dualistic

---

* 'Jargon' in English in the original.

constitution of antagonistic subjectivities. The transformation of labour power from mass worker [*operaio massa*] into social worker [*operaio sociale*] was thus described on the basis of the parameters of analysis of the 'value form' – in other words, not only in relation to the crisis of the measure (magnitude) of value or to the modification of the substance (socialization and immaterialization) of labour, but as a transformation of the very mode of production, that is, of the ensemble of social and political structures that give shape to exploitation and domination. Thus labour opened up to further capacities [*potenze*], from the social worker to the figure we were later to call 'productive multitude', installed on a biopolitical fabric. The space of capitalist exploitation and social resistance was also expanded, to the point of configuring itself at the global level, while exploitation extended its grip over the whole of society (namely to the extraction of value from social production – later on).

The progressive lexical revolution that so-called post-*operaismo* produced (from 'mass worker' to 'social worker' to 'multitude') reflected the transformations of real being; it was ontologically founded. So let's go back to that unspeakable word, 'ontology'. Why be afraid of this word – the analysis of being as being – when it is evident that, for materialists, it delivers nothing but the materialist lesson of being as production? Who is afraid of ontology, when it is defined as an ontology of production and therefore of social antagonisms? Only those who do not manage to be radically materialist will have reason to be afraid. Now, 'ontologically grounded' means three things here. The first is that history, determinate being, is the inescapable basis of any struggle for liberation, that the struggles of the proletariat, victorious or defeated, are left behind in history, and that history is variously composed of these determinations. This hard historical foundation, which constitutes the materialist terrain of our analysis, is what is defined in the 'form' of value, taken in Isaak Illich Rubin's sense (but also that of the young Marx and of historical materialism).

The second point is that this ontology is dualistic, antagonistic. It develops in the class struggle, and thus invests the capital relation according to biopolitical dimensions. It is life put to work and life subjected to dominion that clash here continually, and the ontology is marked and never resolved by this clash. Hence the illusory nature of any 'escape route' that wants to explode the capital relation in an imaginary *jetztzeit*, in instantaneous, event-like fashion. No, we must work on this relationship, with continuity, in order to open it to liberation. What is the socialization of production mobilizes is the whole terrain of reproduction. We have to work this ontology so that the exploited, the workers, the poor, and the excluded will have the strength not only to subvert our world but also to reinvent it.

And here emerges the third point of this ontology: the constituent *dispositif*. In antagonism, subjective forces are formed; in history, subjectivity is produced – because the production of subjectivity is a 'production of production'; it is the very development of history, seen by the struggles and in the ability to construct – with the subjectivities themselves – wealth and freedom. In this materialism being is never empty, never impotent; it is always traversed by work and desire, that is, by the productivity of living labour. Herein lies the main conflict of any history of metaphysics – that between the materialist conception of productive being and the mystical–transcendental conception of negative being; and here comes to the fore the need to choose between Hobbes and Spinoza, between fascism and freedom. That same 'fear' – which, according to Hobbes, is at the foundation of the transcendental sovereign – in fact has a second and truer definition, which is at the foundation of our own civilisation: the constructive fear, the one remembered in 'the year 1000' – the fear that the people of Europe, arising from the barbarism of the Middle Ages, had the ability to overcome, decisively opposing the superstition and the destructive myth that underpins it. They cast themselves – even though poor, exploited and excluded – beyond the margins of fear, superstition and domination, to build civilization.

Post-*operaismo*, then? And why ever 'post-'? What was built in the prisons, and then taken out to organize the struggles in the overlap into the new century, was rather a new version of *operaismo*, in the continuity of its ontological foundation and method. Decisive in it (as in the workerist practices of the 1960s) were the conception of class struggles as being constructive, the [practice of] inquiry, and an antagonistic analysis of the historical process. And then there was simply the adaptation of that matrix to the new reality – an 'updating' to the new forms of the historical condition. *Operaismo* as an ontology? Yes, because ontology is the only possibility of saying what we are and what we want to be; because ontology is being productive, and without production there is no life. Thus we emerged from the crude *operaismo* shaped between *Quaderni rossi* and *Classe operaia* and, while *operaismo* was feeding on the results of past struggles, it also opened up to future struggles.

So how did this *operaismo* come to terms with the new class composition? How did it develop and update the crude approach of the 1960s? What were its fundamental concepts, and what were the contaminations from contemporary thought that it had to address and by which it was fertilized? In what follows I can do no more than draw a list of the subsequent updatings of this development, and therefore of the capacity of *operaismo* to continue having a grip on the reality of class conflict and gradually to define its changing subjects.

A first episode is linked to the discovery of the factory-society. But, in the 1970s, this was not because the factory extended into society, as had happened since the beginning of the twentieth century, but because society began to absorb the factory. The struggles of the 1960s had greatly weakened capitalist command within factories; the workers' struggle had been impossible to contain. It was then that, beginning with a strong capitalist counterattack, the factories were largely deconstructed and shifted to new locations: we witnessed industrial automation and a major reduction in the workforces employed, the outsourcing of secondary production departments, and a reorganization of territories in productive terms. The walls of the factories had collapsed, and mobility and flexibility became the defining qualities of a workforce that had become completely socialized and forced into precarity (or was swallowed into unemployment). Industry became socialized, and so did the worker: the 'social worker', who succeeded the 'mass worker', was waiting to fuse into the 'multitude' of singularities that, between education and factory, between services and unemployment, sought a new location in the social networks of production. It was necessary to understand all this at a time when the forces of the left – political and trade union alike – were unable to do so and were still fixated on the old figures of labour, imagining that those could be defended through corporatism, and thereby losing all capacity to express the new technical composition of socialized labour power and to lead an attack on the ongoing capitalist restructuring. The *operaisti* tried to intervene in this transition but were defeated. They will never forgive the political and trade union forces of the left for not having been at the workers' side in this transitional period, having chosen instead to be internal to the capitalist 'reforms'.

From a theoretical point of view, the Marxian distinction between a 'formal' and a 'real' subsumption underwent a development here, the former referring to the relative subordination of labour (and society) under capital, the latter referring to the becoming total of that subordination. The analysis of this transition is what characterized the first period of *operaismo*. But already in the 1970s this dimension could be questioned, because the 'real' subsumption was shaken by the modification of the form of labour – and in particular by the emergence of immaterial labour. Immaterial labour means intellectual, cooperative and affective labour, together with the kind of labour that takes place in a non-repetitive way, in services and in industry; thus it also includes material labour, organized in digitalized forms or in servicing automation. Immaterial labour accepted the real subsumption of society under capital as a precondition; however, it envisaged a redevelopment of the overall framework into a new postindustrial regime of production, built on networks created via the computerization of work and society.

Secondly, therefore, the analysis of the new technical composition of labour also underwent a development. In other words, a question arose. How did labour power – variable capital in its relation to fixed capital – change in the transition from the industrial to the postindustrial mode of production, from Fordist material labour to post-Fordist immaterial labour? The answer had already been glimpsed, in the early 1960s, in the analyses offered by various comrades of the *Quaderni rossi* group (Romano Alquati and Ferruccio Gambino in particular) who, in studying the development of struggles in the most advanced factories, had understood the progressive prevalence of intelligence over bodies in the production process. These early signs were to find support in the reading of the 'Fragment on Machines' in Marx's *Grundrisse* – which made it possible to cast Marx's general intellect as the object of the inquiry. Hence new definitions of the productivity of living labour in its immateriality – intelligent, affective and so on – and of the forms in which capital organized it. But we also had the first experiences of the ways in which this new labour organized resistance – for it was not true that mass intellectual labour, the 'mass intellectuality', was more easily subjected to capital. Indeed, it contained an energy that matched resistance with the ability to project an 'other'. But I shall come to that shortly.

For the moment, let us remember how important the analysis of labour cooperation became here. We know that the study of cooperation is essential to the definition of productivity – in production, cooperation always brings about an excess of value. Now cooperation was enormously incentivized by the fact that it was given in the immaterial expression of labour. Labour, by becoming cognitive, by connecting to the Internet and so on, acquired a powerful transversality. The strong cooperation established between these expressive powers showed a potential of autonomy and singularization, of 'difference' and resistance, in the face of, and against, capitalist command. It will be clear how much the figure of virtuality, of expressive power, of difference and excess, owes to the work of Deleuze and Guattari. It was in fact an explicit contamination that came about through discussions of *A Thousand Plateaus*. If the social worker became a cognitive worker, the social qualities of the former – mobility, flexibility, and the like – were combined with the cognitive qualities of the latter: transversality, linguistic cooperation, and so forth. If the social worker had introduced the factory into the social, the cognitive worker built a social enterprise of communicating as the basis of production.

From intelligence to life: this was, then, the step to take. In fact, once the cognitive worker was defined, one wondered – having recorded the capitalist attempt to subsume general intellect – where value was now created; and one recognized that it arose precisely from the exploitation of social cooperation, of the reproductive networks of the social, and from that common element between the 'private' and the 'public' appropriation of value that the mode of production presupposed. It was on this point that *operaismo* had to be further updated, when it was felt that the socialization of production and cognitive activity infused life. The technical composition of labour opened up to forms of life, and it was these that became decisive in the process of production. Life was put to work; and this meant that not only the world of production but also that of reproduction (which includes the reproduction of life) was put to work. The new working subjects – mobile, flexible, social and cognitive – and the form of life that was distinctly theirs turned out to be biopolitical figures, bioproductive and reproductive of *bios* [life].

The importance that feminist movements, mobilized on the terrain of social reproduction, had in redefining social production and the form of life itself, as a decisive element of production, is completely obvious. On this terrain, too, the struggles were the first to give expression to this modification of the social (and perhaps political) composition of the proletariat: the feminist movement had an epistemological as well as a pedagogic efficacy. And *operaismo* made the biopolitical understanding of the production of value into a new axis of research, which was to lead it to two outcomes. The first was the ability to gather, under the antagonistic definition of capital, every form of exploitation given on the social terrain. With this they took on board (critically) third-worldist conceptions, which up to that point had been capable only of dramatizing the particular, pulling together the instances of emancipation and the specificity of anti-imperialist protest in the unity of the anticapitalist project. The second outcome was indeed to bestow antagonistic dignity on social movements in their struggles – far more broadly than the old socialist organizations would have been able to do – which were embarking on hypocritical policies of 'alliances' for this purpose. And it was also to rediscover here, in these struggles, that point of view that had created *operaismo* and to be able to adopt it in the here and now: to see every historical development of the struggle for liberation from work from below, from the class struggle of the exploited. This involved the ability to give this point of view biopolitical intensity and a universal extension. Once the centrality of the factory was over, class struggle regained here completely its revolutionary potential.

Having reached this point, it was time for us to enquire into the political composition of this new proletariat. It was like submitting it to an *experimentum crucis* [decisive test] in order to bring out a new subjective figure sturdy enough to sustain a *constituent power*, because this was the 'new' that the series of updates conducted until then could graft onto *operaismo*. The idea was to make it not a 'post-' (which is always a pejorative, if not a corrupting prefix) but a 'new' *operaismo* – which could recover the freshness and theoretical power of the *operaismo* of the 1960s – the 'old' *operaismo*. There was here in the new an element of strong innovativeness by comparison with the old: the point where, as already mentioned, an excess of cooperative or cognitive labour broke the old triadic sequence of struggles–crisis–restructuring, which had been classic for a while. Here, when this excedence, this power [*potenza*] was grasped in the new political composition of the proletariat and had an effect on the level of political innovation and the repetition of the triad struggles–crisis–restructuring was crushed. Already in the phenomenological background of the analysis, living labour contained in embryo that constructive power that expressed itself fully as *constituency*. And one recognized in living labour an institutional and creative yearning, in no way imitative or parasitic (like that energy of the working class in the old *operaismo*, comfortably ensconced in the authoritarian structures of Third Internationalism). If, then, living labour had revealed through inquiry its co-essentiality with social cooperation, and if cooperation, combined with communication, revealed the extraordinary productivity of its immaterial connections; if the genealogy of general intellect had offered a seminal paradigm to these theoretical developments, we could now go further. We could immerse this living labour in history and identify the processes of subjectivation, of *constitution*, that made it a political subject.

Could this hypothesis of a possible constitution of the political composition of the proletariat, in close continuity with the definition of technical composition, be open to criticism? As if there were a necessary and compelling connection between one and the other? Yes, of course. The insistence exercised here on political subjectivity gave an impression of ideal abstraction and improper ontological fixation. It seemed that, simply through the force of logic, the conclusion of the reasoning was implicit in its premise – exactly the sort of thing that a materialist investigation cannot permit. It is clear, then, that here it was necessary to advance and describe processes of subjectivation capable of taking apart every assumption and of restoring them entirely to praxis.

At this point it was necessary to reconnect with history and to compare the hypotheses against the historical process. The danger of an abstract codification of the experience could be averted only by historicizing the analysis carried out up until then and by undertaking to describe the subjectivation of living labour within its material realization. Foucault was extremely useful here, because he supplied the means to translate historical analysis into a constituent experience, through a genealogical approach and a definitive new articulation of politics and ethics – in short, through a return to militancy as the basis of every 'truth' and to collective resistance as the basis of every behaviour and every political conquest. This immersion in the historicity of the struggles was in no way an individualist operation: the conditions of a collective constitution of the subject were in fact given. They come when militancy is recognized as an excavation of the 'we', as a destitution [*destituzione*, taking down] of individuality and a strong focus on 'making truth'. It is clear that this brings us back to *operaismo* as a place from which it is possible to build political movement and in which we recognise ourselves in the movement for political liberation.

It is not just an ethical–political decision. This transition is also a means to knowledge, because the first consequence of what I have tried to show so far, namely the new historical ontology of the working-class struggle against exploitation, puts us in the situation of confronting command ourselves – of setting ourselves up against capital, as living labour. The story that each one of us is obliged to live and in which we seek liberation is one internal to class struggle. How can we organize our life in this confrontation? How can we place ourselves within or against capitalist command, recognizing that we have no alternative, fighting it, blocking its force of exploitation of the individual and of collective extraction of value – snatching from it the tools of knowledge and power? I would say that these questions lie at the heart of *operaismo*. These were the questions that mass workers raised in the factory when they organized their resistance, and they are the questions that we ask ourselves in our struggle to free ourselves, in the context of a domination [*dominio*] imposed on us in general intellect. We are within capitalist command, we live in it; it is within these ontological conditions that we put to work the desire for liberation – this is the place where a postmodern Machiavelli would go in order to build a revolutionary alternative.

I think that I should close here the list of categories that characterize *operaismo* in its various redactions. I would like simply to mention a few themes that are at the centre of discussions among *operaisti* today. First, of course, the theme of globalization. Groups of comrades continue to work on it, closely linking the analysis of geopolitical relations to that of the new structurings and movements in the global labour market. The problem of migration, understood as one of the current forms of class struggle, is at the core of this chapter. Next comes the theme of the common, in other words the radical critique of private and public property: a third element has inserted itself at the base of the analysis of the conditions of production, into the relationship between forces of production and relations of production (which always deliver the former to exploited living labour and the latter to the functions of organization and command): the common subjectivation of the mode of production. In the class struggle, the strength of workers is advanced through the appropriation of quotas of fixed capital – or, better, by taking away from general capital certain margins of power over the organization of production. This is the common, which appears here as a consolidated ontological deposit and today opens itself to new achievements. This opening yields another field of analysis, related to the new forms in which the revolutionary struggle is organized today. We live *within* capital and are *against* its command: in these conditions the struggle will always be a combination of exodus and desertion. Desertion from command and exodus beyond command are the two lines that *operaismo* always keeps to the fore in the theory of organization. But all this is only a taste of the themes treated by *operaismo* today. What a long way we have come, upholding this method!

What, then, is post-*operaismo*? Put simply, it doesn't exist. This strange way of naming the theoretical and political work begun in the 1960s by autonomous communist militants, massified in the 1970s, then developed in the prisons of the republic and, later still, turned into an international body of research came into use only in the second decade of this century. And, paradoxically, the ones who began to use this 'post-' prefix were those who had not wanted to have anything to do with *operaismo* since the end of the 1960s. Since then, these comrades who abandoned *operaismo* developed their thinking by reconnecting to the reactionary current of modern political thought that runs from Hobbes to Carl Schmitt. Onto their 'raw' *operaismo* they implanted old socialist orientations and allowed themselves finally to drift into sovereignist and populist options. One may conclude that the only post-*operaista* nowadays (and one with no large following) is Mario Tronti, and that the thinking of those thousands of comrades who have gone on to develop the raw principle of the working class point of view can legitimately assume and defend the name '*operaismo*' – just so, *tout court*, without bells and whistles.

And now, to conclude. This story is written by just one person among those thousands. He makes no claim to represent them. With some of them he shares almost all of what has been said here; with others he openly disagrees on some points, or indeed many. But there is one thing that unites them all, these *operaisti*. And it is the fact that *operaismo* is the method of reconstructing a class power that, as soon as it becomes possible, might revolutionize this stultified world of exploitation and injustice that we inhabit.

Notes

Note to Chapter 1

1 See M. Cacciari, *Krisis*, Feltrinelli: Milan 1978. [Massimo Cacciari was a member of the Italian Communist Party from 1969: translator's note.]

Notes to Chapter 2

1 See A. Negri, 'Keynes and the capitalist theory of the state post 1929' [1972], in idem, *Revolution Retrieved: Selected Writings on Marx, Keynes, Capitalist Crisis and New Social Subjects, 1967–83*, ed. and trans. by E. Emery, Red Notes: London 1988, pp. 5–42.
2 See Institut für Gesellschaftswissenschaften beim ZK der SED, *Imperialismus heute: Der staatsmonopolistische Kapitalismus in West-deutschland*, Dietz: Berlin 1967; R. Gündel et al., *Zur Theorie des staatsmonopolistischen Kapitalismus*, Verlag DEB – Das Europäischer Buch: Berlin 1967; Comité Central PCF (ed.), *Le capitalisme mono-poliste d'état*, Éditions Sociales: Paris 1971; Autoren-Kollektiv, *Der Imperialismus der BRD*, Dietz: Berlin 1971. See also various writings by P. Boccara published by the Central Committee of the French Communist Party.
3 P. A. Baran and P. M. Sweezy, *Monopoly Capitalism*, Monthly Review Press: New York 1966, p. 67; P. Jalée, *Imperialism in the Seventies*, Third Press: New York 1972. The reference here is to pp. 133–44 in the Italian translation.
4 N. Poulantzas, *Political Power and Social Classes*, New Left Books: London 1973, p. 273.
5 E. Varga, *Essais sur l'économie politique du capitalisme*, Foreign Language Editions: Moscow 1967. See especially E. Varga, *Die Krise des Kapitalismus und ihre politischen Folgen*, ed. by E. Altvater, Europäische Verlagsanstalt: Frankfurt 1969.

6 S. L. Wygodski, *Der gegenwärtige Kapitalismus: Versuch einer theoretischen Analyse*, Pahl-Rugenstein Verlag: Cologne 1972, esp. p. 9.

7 G. Lukács clearly defined the structural, objective intensity of mechanisms of legality in his *History and Class Consciousness*, MIT Press: Cambridge 1971.

8 In general, and specifically on the critique of stamocap, see M. Wirth, *Kapitalismustheorie in der DDR: Entstehung und Entwicklung der Theorie des staatsmonopolistischen Kapitalismus*, Suhrkamp: Frankfurt 1972; M. Wirth, *Monopol und Staat: Zur Marx-Rezeption in der Theorie des staats-monopolistischen Kapitalismus*, ed. by R. Ebbinghausen, Suhrkamp: Frankfurt 1974. In this collection, see especially the articles by R. Winkelmann, pp. 45–97, and W. Tristram, pp. 98–136.

9 Hence the formidably repressive effect of theories of stamocap in socialist countries: see M. Wirth, *Monopol und Staat*, pp. 27ff.

10 See Wygodski, *Der gegenwärtige Kapitalismus*, and especially the references in Wirth, *Monopol und Staat*.

11 See the Introduction by R. Ebbinghausen and R. Winkelmann in Wirth, *Monopol und Staat*.

12 Interesting in this regard is the controversy that arose in the Communist Party of France during the 1974 Congress, a controversy that saw – against the party line and against the likes of Herzog – a first attitude against stamocap theories taken by sectors of the party more tied to the organization of the working class. The Althusserian left has attempted an interpretation of this polemical point of view, attacking the orthodoxy of Althusser himself. See especially the essay by É. Balibar, 'Plus-value et classes sociales', in idem, *Cinq études du materialisme historique*, Maspéro: Paris 1974.

13 K. Marx and F. Engels, *Manifesto of the Communist Party*, Foreign Languages Press: Peking, 1965, p. 35.

14 For a general coverage, see R. Guastini, *Marx: Dalla filosofia del diritto alla scienza della società*, Il Mulino: Bologna 1974.

15 K. Marx and F. Engels, *The German Ideology*, Progress Publishers: Moscow 1976, p. 99.

16 K. Marx, *Grundrisse*, Vintage Books: New York 1973, p. 108.

17 A. Negri, 'Rileggendo Pasukanis: Note di discussione', *Critica del diritto* 1 (1974): 90–119.

18 Letter from Marx to Lassalle, 22 February 1858, from K. Marx, *Selected Correspondence*, International Publishers: New York 1942, p. 96.

19 K. Marx, *Capital*, International Publishers: New York 1967, vol. 3, p. 438.

20 F. Engels, *Antidühring*, Progress Publishers: Moscow, 1969, p. 330.

21 Engels, *Antidühring*, p. 330 (also for the next two quotations); translation slightly modified.

22 R. Finzi, 'Lo stato del capitale: Un problema aperto', *Studi storici* 11.3 (1970): 488–508, here pp. 491–2.

23 Marx, *Grundrisse*, p. 264.
24 See S. Bologna, P. Carpignano, and A. Negri, *Crisi e organizzazione operaia*, Feltrinelli: Milan 1974.
25 Marx, *Grundrisse*, pp. 101–2.
26 R. Miliband, *The State in Capitalist Society*, Basic Books: New York, 1969. For Ralph Miliband, see also R. Miliband, 'Marx and the state' [1965], *Marxist Critique* 4.2 (1966): 91–112.
27 N. Poulantzas, *Political Power and Social Classes*, New Left Books: London 1973.
28 N. Poulantzas, 'The problem of the capitalist state', *New Left Review* 58 (1969): 67–78; all the quotations that follow here are from p. 70. R. Miliband, 'The capitalist state: Reply to Nicos Poulantzas', *New Left Review* 59 (1970): 53–60. See also H. G. Haupt and S. Liebfried, 'Anmerkung zur Controverse Poulantzas-Miliband', *Kritische Justiz* 4.2 (1971): 217–34. https://www.kj.nomos.de/archiv/1971-4/heft-2-133-240.
29 See G. Guastini, 'Teoria e fenomenologia dello stato capitalistico', *Politica del diritto* 6 (1971): 781–806.
30 A. Serafini, 'Gramsci e la conquista dello stato', *Compagni* 1.2–3 (1970): 39–40.
31 See Finzi, 'Lo stato del capitale, and Guastini, 'Teoria e fenomenologia'.
32 On this methodology, see L. Althusser and E. Balibar, *Reading* Capital, New Left Books: London 1970; also L. Althusser, *For Marx*, Verso: London 1996.
33 For the critique of Althusserian methodology, see P. A. Rovatti, *Critica e scientificità in Marx*, Feltrinelli: Milan 1973; J. Rancière, *L'ideologia politica in Althusser*, Feltrinelli: Milan 1974.
34 F. H. Cardoso, in N. Poulantzas and F. H. Cardoso, *Sul concetto di classe*, Feltrinelli: Milan 1974, p. 56. But see also Rancière, *L'ideologia politica*.
35 Cardoso, in N. Poulantzas and F. H. Cardoso, *Sul concetto di classe*, Feltrinelli: Milan 1974, p. 62.
36 For a critique of Gramsci's theory of civil society carried out from a Marxian point of view, see N. Bobbio, 'Gramsci e la concezione della società civile', in *Gramsci e la cultura contemporanea: Atti del Convegno internazionale di studi marxiani tenuto a Cagliari il 23–27 aprile 1967*, ed. by P. Rossi, Editori Riuniti: Rome 1969, vol. 1.
37 A. Pizzorno, 'Sul metodo di Gramsci: Dalla storiografia alla scienza politica', *Quaderni di sociologia* 16.7 (1967): 380–400.
38 N. Poulantzas, 'Préliminaires à l'étude de l'hégémonie dans l'état', *Temps modernes* 234 (1965): 862–96 and 235 (1965): 1048–69.
39 R. Luxemburg, *Politische Schriften*, Europe Verlag: Vienna 1966, vol. 1, p. 76.
40 Two examples are R. Rosdolsky, *Genesi e struttura del 'Capitale' di Marx*, Laterza: Bari 1971 and H. Reichelt, *La struttura logica del concetto di capitale in Marx*, Laterza: Bari 1973.

41 W. Müller and C. Neusüß, 'Die Sozialstaatsillusion und der Widerspruch von Lohnarbeit und Kapital', *PROKLA: Zeitschrift für Kritische Sozialwissenschaft* 1.1 (1971): 7–70, here p. 9. https://doi.org/10.32387/prokla.v1iSonderheft.1117.

42 Müller and Neusüss, 'Die Sozialistaatsillusion', pp. 43–4; see also M. Tronti, *Workers and Capital*, Verso: London 2019.

43 Marx, *Grundrisse*, p. 97.

44 R. Panzieri, *La ripresa del marxismo-leninismo in Italia*, ed. by D. Lanzardo, Sapere: Milan 1972.

45 For the journal *Quaderni rossi*, see its complete reprint by Sapere Edizioni in Milan.

46 See esp. the collections of *Classe operaia* (1964–7), *Contropiano* (1968–), *Potere operaio* (1969–73) and *Il Manifesto* (monthly).

47 In the absence of more recent adequate treatments of the problem, Marx's *Grundrisse* and 'Unpublished Chapter VI' unfortunately remain the first port of call on these themes.

48 A Negri, 'Crisis of the planner state: Communism and revolutionary organisation', in idem, *Revolution Retrieved*, pp. 91–148.

49 J. Habermas, *The Structural Transformation of the Public Sphere: An Inquiry into a Category of Bourgeois Society*, Polity: Cambridge 1989.

50 H. J. Krahl, *Costituzione e lotta di classe*, Jaca Book: Milan 1973; R. Dutschke, V. Bergmann, W. Lefevre, and R. Rabehl, *La ribellione degli studenti*, Feltrinelli: Milan 1968.

51 C. Offe, 'Dominio politico e struttura di classe', *Rassegna italiana di sociologia* 12.1 (1971): 47–82, here p. 73 See especially the set of articles in C. Offe, *Strukturprobleme des kapitalistischen Staates: Aufsätze zur politischen Soziologie*, Suhrkamp: Frankfurt 1972, 1973.

52 Offe, 'Dominio politico', p. 73 (also for the next three quotations in this paragraph).

53 In particular by the writers of the so-called 'pessimistic school'. See especially P. Bachrach and M. S. Baratz, *Power and Poverty*, Oxford University Press: Oxford 1970 and E. E. Schattscheider, *The Semi-Sovereign People*, Holt-Reinhart and Winston: New York 1960.

54 An explicit classist indication, starting from the analytical assumptions of these methodological approaches, can be found in J. Huffschmid, *Die Politik des Kapitals: Konzentration und Wirtschaftspolitik in der Bundesrepublik*, Suhrkamp: Frankfurt 1969 and in various articles in *Scienze politiche: Enciclopedia Feltrinelli Fischer*, ed. by A. Negri, Feltrinelli: Milan 1970.

55 J. Agnoli, *Die Transformation der Demokratie und verwandte Schriften*, Konkret: Hamburg 2004; J. Agnoli, 'Die bürgerliche Gesellschaft und ihr Staat', *Das Argument* 41 (1966) , 449–61; J. Agnoli, 'Strategia rivoluzionaria e parlamentarismo', in *Sviluppo economico e rivoluzione*, ed. by F. Ayamone, A. Sivini Cavazzani and G. Sivini, De Donato: Bari 1969.

56 W. Euchner, 'Zur Lage des Parlamentarismus', in *Der CDU-Staat: Analysen zur Verfassungswirklichkeit der Bundesrepublik*, ed. by G. Schafer and C. Nedelmann, Suhrkamp: Frankfurt 1969, vol. 1, pp. 105–32.

57 H. J. Blank and J. Kirsch, 'Vom Elend des Gesetzgebers', in *Der CDU-Staat: Analysen zur Verfassungswirklichkeit der Bundesrepublik*, ed. by G. Schafer and C. Nedelmann, Suhrkamp: Frankfurt 1969, vol. 1, pp. 133–75. A. Negri, 'Alcune riflessioni sullo "stato dei partiti"', *Rivista trimestrale di diritto pubblico* 1 (1964): 1–60.

58 Here we could add an appendix on an article by L. Althusser, 'Ideologia e apparati ideologici di stato', *Critica marxista* 5 (1970): 23–65, since – leaving aside the major methodological discrepancies – it deals with a similar theme and resolves it by going in a similar direction.

59 J. Hirsch, *Wissenschaftlich-technischer Fortschritt und politisches System: Organisation und Grundlagen administrativer Wissenschaftsförderung in der BRD*, Suhrkamp: Frankfurt 1970.

60 See also J. Kirsch, 'Elemente einer materialistischen Staatstheorie', in *Probleme einer materialistischen Staatstheorie*, ed. by C. von Braunmühl, K. Funken, M. Cagoy and J. Kirsch, Suhrkamp: Frankfurt 1973, pp. 199–266; also two of the same author's articles published in *Politikwissenschaft: Eine Einfuhrung in ihre Probleme*, ed. by G. Kress and D. Senghaas, Europäische Verlagsanstalt: Frankfurt 1969.

61 Jim O'Connor, *The Fiscal Crisis of the State*, St Martin's Press: New York 1973.

62 Offe, *Strukturprobleme*, esp. pp. 169ff; also C. Offe, 'Krisen des Krisen-management: Elemente einer politischen Krisentheorie', in *Herrschaft und Krise*, ed. by M. Jaenicke, Westdeutscher Verlag: Opladen 1973, pp. 197–223.

63 On the American experience in general, see the essay by P. Carpignano in Bologna et al., *Crisi e organizzazione operaia*, and some of the works mentioned there, in particular *Regulating the Poor*, ed. by F. Fox Piven and R. Cloward, Random House: New York 1972 and R. Theobald, *Il reddito garantito*, Franco Angeli: Milan 1972.

64 J. Habermas, *Legitimation Crisis*, Polity: Cambridge, 2007.

65 See Offe, *Strukturprobleme*, pp. 27–63.

66 For this critique I draw on S. Sardei-Biermann, J. Christiansen and K. Dohlse, 'Class nomination and politics system: A critical interpretation of recent contributions by Claus Offe', *Kapitalistate* 2 (1973): 60–9.

67 E. Altvater, 'Zu einigen Problemen des Staatsinterventionismus', *Probleme des Klassenkampfs* 2.3 (1972): 1–54 (there is a shorter English version under the title 'Notes on some problems of state intervention-ism', *Kapitalistate* 1 (1973): 96–108 and 2 (1973): 76–83). Along the same lines, see also S. von Flatow and F. Huisken, 'Zum Problem der Ableitung des bürgerlichen Staates', *Probleme des Klassenkampfs* 7 (1973): 83–153, and M. Wirth, 'Zur Kritik der Theorie des Klassenkampfs', *Probleme des Klassenkampfs* 8–9 (1973): 17–44.

68 W. Müller, 'Die Grenzen der Sozialpolitik in der Marktwirtschaft', in *Der CDU-Staat: Analysen zur Verfassungswirklichkeit der Bundesrepublik*, ed. by G. Schafer and C. Nedelmann, Suhrkamp: Frankfurt 1969, vol. 1, pp. 14–47.

69 Altvater, 'Zu einigen Problemen'.

70 P. Mattick, *Marx e Keynes: I limiti dell'economia mista*, Laterza: Bari 1969.

71 See sections 2 and 6 in this chapter.

72 See notes in A. Negri, 'Marx on cycle and crisis', in *Revolution Retrieved*, pp. 43–90.

73 See R. Alquati, *Sulla Fiat e altri scritti*, Feltrinelli: Milan 1975 and A. Negri, 'Crisis of the planner state: Communism and revolutionary organisation', in idem, *Revolution Retrieved*, pp. 91–148.

74 The first steps in this direction were the articles contained in *L'operaio multinazionale*, ed. by A. Serafini, Feltrinelli: Milan 1974 and in *Imperialismo e classe operaia multinazionale*, ed. by L. Ferrari Bravo, Feltrinelli: Milan 1975.

75 S. Bologna and A. Negri (eds), *Operai e stato: Lotte operate e riforma dello stato capitalistico tra rivoluzione d'ottobre e New Deal*, Feltrinelli: Milan 1972; H. van der Wee (ed.), *The Great Depression Revisited: Essays on the Economics of the Thirties*, Martinus Nijhoff: The Hague 1972.

76 See G. L. S. Shackle, *Economic Thought, 1926–1939*, Cambridge University Press: Cambridge 1967, and especially H. W. Arndt, *The Economic Lessons of the Nineteen-Thirties*, Routledge: New York 2013; also A. H. Hansen, *Full Recovery or Stagnation?* Norton: New York 1938 and A. H. Hansen, *Fiscal Policy and Business Cycles*, Norton: New York 1941.

77 P. Sraffa, *Production of Commodities by Means of Commodities: Prelude to a Critique of Economic Theory*, Cambridge University Press: Cambridge 1960. Alongside the fundamental work of Sraffa we should also remember that of Nicholas Kaldor, 'The relation of growth and cyclical fluctuations', *Economic Journal* 64.253 (1954): 53–71.

78 C. Napoleoni, in *Il dibattito su Sraffa*, ed. by F. Botta, De Donato: Bari, 1974, p. 52. See also the bibliography offered there.

79 Napoleoni, in *Il dibattito su Sraffa*, ed. by F. Botta, De Donato: Bari, 1974, p. 59.

80 P. Nuti, in *II dibattito su Sraffa*, ed. by F. Botta, De Donato: Bari, 1974, p. 271.

81 On the origins of Keynes's 'idealism', see in particular P. Fabra, '25 ans après Bretton Woods', *Le Monde de l'économie*, 8 July 1969.

82 On these issues, and with useful analytical indications, see V. K. Preuss, *Legalität und Pluralismus: Beiträge zum Verfassungsrecht der BRD*, Suhrkamp: Frankfurt 1973.

83 In general, in this regard, see the latest writers on programming in Italy, as cited by Rescigno in an article published in *Critica del diritto* in 1974. On the success of decisionism, however, see G. Schwab, *The Challenge of*

Exception, Duncker-Humbolt: Berlin, 1970 and J. Freund, *L'essence du politique*, Sirey: Paris, 1965.

84 See O'Connor, *Fiscal Crisis*; P. Brachet, *L'état-patron: Théories et réalités*, F. Cujas: Paris 1974; P. Dubois, *La mort de l'état-patron*, Éditions Ouvrières: Paris, 1974; M. Cogoy, 'Werttheorie und Staatsausgaben', in C. von Braunmühl et al., *Probleme einer materialistischen Staatstheorie*, pp. 129–198.

85 K. H. Roth, *Die 'andere' Arbeiterbewegung und die Entwicklung der kapitalistischen Repression von 1880 bis zur Gegenwart: Ein Beitrag zum Neuverständnis der Klassengeschichte in Deutschland*, Trikont Verlag: Munich, 1974

86 See in this regard, in addition to the fundamental statements of the Italian Communist Party, the comical article by L. Cafagna, 'Classe e stato nello stato di transizione leninista', *Politica e Diritto* 4–5 (1971): 503–29.

87 A useful starting point is D. Zolo, *La teoria comunista dell'estinzione dello Stato*, De Donato: Bari, 1974.

88 See section 6 and n. 69 in this chapter.

Notes to Chapter 3

1 Paul Sweezy, *Theory of Capitalist Development*, Dennis Dobson: London, 1946, p. 33.

2 Sweezy, *Theory of Capitalist Development*.

3 Sweezy, *Theory of Capitalist Development*.

4 Sweezy, *Theory of Capitalist Development*, p. 54.

Notes to Chapter 6

1 Martin Heidegger, *The Question Concerning Technology, and Other Essays*, trans. W. Levitt, Garland: New York 1977, p. 14.

2 K. Marx, *Capital*, vol. 1, trans. Ben Fowkes, Penguin Classics: London, 1990; vol. 2, trans. David Fernbach, Penguin Classics: London, 1991; vol. 3, trans. David Fernbach, Penguin Classics: London, 1991.

3 See C. Vercellone, 'From formal subsumption to general intellect: Elements for a Marxist reading of the thesis of cognitive capitalism', *Historical Materialism* 15.1 (2007): 13–36, and C. Vercellone, 'From the crisis to the "welfare of the common" as a new mode of production', *Theory, Culture & Society* 327–8 (2015): 85–99, doi: 10.1177/02632764 15597770.

4 C. Marazzi, 'L'ammortamento del corpo macchina', *Multitudes* 27 (2007), http://www.multitudes.net/L-ammortamento-del-corpo-macchina.

Notes to Chapter 7

1 All the quotations from this work come from K. Marx, *Grundrisse*, Vintage Books: New York 1973.
2 M. Tronti, *Workers and Capital*, Verso: London 2019, p. 173.
3 See C. Vercellone, 'From formal subsumption to general intellect: Elements for a Marxist reading of the thesis of cognitive capitalism', *Historical Materialism* 15.1 (2007): 13–36, and C. Vercellone, 'From the crisis to the "welfare of the common" as a new mode of production', *Theory, Culture & Society* 32.7–8 (2015): 85–99, doi: 10.1177/0263276415597770. See also Ch. 6, n. 3.
4 C. Marazzi, 'L'ammortamento del corpo macchina', *Multitudes* 27 (2007), http://www.multitudes.net/L-ammortamento-del-corpo-macchina.
5 The anarcho-communist friend is Antonio Casilli, whose recent talks and books all end with the thoughts paraphrased here.

Note to Chapter 8

1 M. Tronti, *Workers and Capital* [1966], trans. D. Broder, Verso: London 2019, p. 276. All quotations and citations in this chapter use this edition.

Notes to Chapter 9

1 M. Tronti, *Workers and Capital*, trans. D. Broder, Verso: London, 2019. All quotations and citations in this chapter use this edition.
2 M. Tronti, *Il demone della politica: Antologia di scritti, 1958–2015*, Il Mulino: Bologna 2017, p. 297.
3 Tronti, *Il demone*, p. 298 (also for the next quotation).
4 Tronti, *Workers and Capital*, p. 305.
5 Tronti, *Workers and Capital*, p. 307 (also for the next quotation).
6 Tronti, *Workers and Capital*, p. 309 (also for the next quotation).
7 M. Tronti, *Il tempo della politica*, Editori Riuniti: Rome 1980; see pp. 382–90. All quotations and citations in this chapter use this edition.
8 Tronti, *Tempo della politica*, p. 408.
9 M. Tronti, 'Karl und Carl', in idem, *La politica al tramonto*, Einaudi: Turin 1998, pp. 549–60. French version (*La politique au crépuscule*) at http://www.lyber-eclat.net/lyber/tronti/politique_au_crepuscule.html.
10 Tronti, 'Karl und Carl', p. 556.
11 Homer, *Iliad* 1.1–3.
12 Sandro Mezzadra and Brett Neilson, 'Introduction to *The Politics of Operations: Excavating Contemporary Capitalism*', *Euronomade*, 12 January 2019, http://www.euronomade.info/?p=11591. (The original book was published by Duke University Press in the same year.)